ALEX QUICK is the pseudonym of an English novelist. He is the author of *102 Free Things to Do, 102 Ways to Write a Novel, 102 Ways to Improve your Partner, 102 English Things to Do* and *102 Things to Do in Summer.* There will be more...

102
THINGS TO DO
IN AUTUMN

Also by Alex Quick

102 Free Things to Do
102 Ways to Write a Novel
102 English Things to Do
102 Ways to Improve your Partner
102 Things to Do in Winter
102 Things to Do in Spring
102 Things to Do in Summer

First published in 2013 by Old Street Publishing Ltd,
Trebinshun House, Brecon LD3 7PX
www.oldstreetpublishing.co.uk

ISBN 978 1 908699 37 4

10 9 8 7 6 5 4 3 2 1

A CIP catalogue record for this title is available from the British Library.

Printed and bound in Great Britain

*Many thanks to Jeannine, James
and Rob of Gatsby's*

102
THINGS TO DO
IN AUTUMN

ALEX QUICK

CONTENTS

1.

WATCH STARLING MURMURATIONS

On autumn evenings, dark clouds begin to gather. But these clouds do not presage rain. They are clouds of living things: starlings. These birds have a talent for the extraordinary aerial ballets known as 'murmurations'. Thousands of them take to the skies and begin swooping over the landscape with rapid, breathtaking synchrony. As if guided by a single mind, they form cascading, pulsating masses, gather into clumps and clusters that constantly interact, shift and merge. It's one of nature's most extraordinary spectacles.

Why do they do it? There are several theories. One is that it's a defence against predators such as sparrowhawks or peregrine falcons. Predators are confused by the dancing displays and find it hard to focus on any particular bird. Another theory is that it's a form of social behaviour, a way of sharing information about roosting opportunities or food. The truth is that no one knows for sure. Neither is it understood quite how birds separated by hundreds of feet seem to be able to change direction in perfect accord.

In autumn – from November onwards – starling murmurations begin, and they continue into winter. As the days shorten, native birds are swollen by migrants, creating the most spectacular displays. Popular sites to see starlings in the UK include Brighton Pier in Sussex and the Avalon Marshes in Somerset, where a million birds regularly take to the skies. Starling displays can be seen throughout Europe too, particularly in Italy.

Perhaps the mystery will be unravelled one day, but for now, it's enough just to watch and wonder.

2.

GET TO KNOW THE AUTUMN NIGHT SKY

If you don't know much about observing the stars, two things will help. First of all, get as far away from city lights as possible. Secondly, take a pair of binoculars. An expensive telescope is really not necessary to enjoy the stars, and binoculars are cheap, portable and manoeuvrable.

The night sky in autumn offers many interesting sights. The Plough (or Big Dipper) is probably the most familiar constellation, with its shape like a ladle: in autumn in the northern hemisphere it is low down and to the north. If you use it as a marker you can find many other points in the night sky. Start by drawing an imaginary line through the two stars on the right side of the cup of the ladle, and extend the line upwards. The first star you come to is Polaris, the north star, around which all the other stars turn. Keep following the line up and you will come to Cassiopeia, perhaps the most recognisable constellation in the autumn sky: this forms a 'W' on its side. Now turn your attention to the south: here the main autumn constellation is Pegasus, which is an almost perfect square bounded to the right by several outlying legs. With binoculars it's possible to see several galaxies and galactic clusters in and around Pegasus.

Of course that's just the start. There are binary stars, blue-white supergiants, variable stars, globular clusters, supernovae and nebulae. The fine crisp nights of autumn are an ideal time to see and appreciate them.

3.

GORGE ON STINGING NETTLE SOUP

Stinging nettles are full of vitamins and minerals, and as long as you avoid the stings, they will generally make you live longer. However, you don't need to force them down like medicine. Nettles actually taste pretty good, rather like spinach with a hint of seafood. In fact, if you make nettle soup you will notice a rich, mouth-watering aroma, similar to boiling mussels.

It's best to use the young leaves for nettle soup. Nettles will put on new growth in autumn, so have a look for some plants with fresh-looking tips. Wearing gloves, pluck the top six inches or so of each plant, collecting enough to fill a carrier bag loosely.

There are many recipes for nettle soup, some of which sound like the proverbial 'stone soup'; however, the nettles are not the useless magic stone, but a delicious ingredient in their own right. Try this recipe:

Strip the leaves from the stalks, wash them and chop them. Now melt a generous knob of butter in a saucepan and add the nettles, softening them until they reduce and turn dark green. Add two medium-sized potatoes, chopped into cubes, and four soup-bowl's worth of lightly flavoured stock. Simmer for fifteen minutes. Finally, puree the broth in a blender. Serve with a swirl of cream and some black pepper.

Final tip: you can also make soup from dead nettles, the flowering cousins of stinging nettles. The flowers are also edible.

4.

GO TO AN OKTOBERFEST

Oktoberfest is the carnival of lager, lederhosen, dirndls, pretzels, weisswurst and tubas held every year at the Theresienwiese in Munich, Germany. It is attended by around six-and-a-half million people annually. Generally, it's a relaxed and civilised celebration of Germanic culture, but since the beer at Oktoberfest is around 25% stronger than most other beers generally on sale, it also leads to the prolific creation of *Bierleichen*, or beer corpses – people lying on the ground in a drunken stupor.

One of the important things to note about the Oktoberfest is that it's not actually in October (though it is in autumn). It starts in mid-September and runs for sixteen days until the first Sunday in October, unless that first Sunday is before October 2nd, in which case it ends on October 3rd. Either way, the majority of Oktoberfest is always in September, so don't wait until October to book tickets to Germany.

Oktoberfest is now a global franchise. The majority of Oktoberfest revelling, in terms of sheer numbers of people, is now held outside Germany. Oktoberfest-inspired celebrations take place in Canada, the USA, Australia, Argentina, Colombia, Chile, Brazil and Palestine, and so this autumn there is likely to be an Oktoberfest near you. One of the biggest is the Oktoberfest of Blumenau in Brazil, in which nigh on a million people celebrate Brazil's Germanic heritage with events such as 'Metre Drinking', or downing a metre of beer in the shortest time (ladies' and men's events).

5.

TAKE PART IN A CONKER ALIEN MOTH SURVEY

You may have noticed that horse chestnut trees are gaining their autumn colours earlier than usual. This is because of a new parasite, the alien leaf miner moth, *Cameraria ohridella*. First described in 1984 in Macedonia, the moth has spread rapidly throughout Europe, at a rate of around 80km per year, and is now endemic in Austria, Switzerland, France, Germany, the Low Countries and the southern half of the UK.

The Cameraria ohridella's modus operandi is to lay eggs on the leaves of horse chestnut trees; when the eggs hatch, the caterpillars eat little tunnels through the leaves (thus 'leaf miner'). These make the leaves turn brown, and give the trees an autumnal appearance any time from June onwards. It is not thought that the moth endangers the long-term health of the trees it colonises; nevertheless, researchers are interested in the way the moth is spreading, and have invited the public to help record damage.

To do this you need to go to www.conkertreescience. org.uk and register as a conker tree observer. Researchers are looking for several things: what proportion of the leaves are infected; whether birds are taking advantage of the extra meals of caterpillars; whether there is leaf-litter under the tree (which can harbour moths); and so on. Even a report of a healthy tree is useful as it gives an indication that the moth has not yet penetrated into that locale.

6.

GO TO A FARMERS' MARKET

In our great-great-grandparents' time, all food was seasonal. There was rhubarb in March, cherries in July and quinces in December. Nowadays all food is omni-available. Cherries in February? The shelves of your supermarket will groan with them at your command.

This isn't a bad thing *per se*, but there are some costs involved. One is air freight. Those cherries will have travelled a long way to get here, may have polluted the environment as they did so, and may not be very fresh.

At a farmers' market, however, the concept of seasonality returns. Here you find foods that are fresh and locally grown. They have travelled only a few miles to get to you and will be tastier as a result. They may also be more nutritious: food that is stale or old can decline markedly in nutritive value.

At a farmers' market you will also find foods that are available nowhere else in the world. Cheeses of staggering originality; breads by artisan bakers; meats cured, smoked, salted, sausaged, or otherwise crafted in traditional ways. And they may be cheaper than at supermarket prices, especially if you turn up at the end of the day when producers are unloading their remaining stock.

Autumn, naturally, is the time to go. In temperate zones, most fruits and vegetables come into season in the autumn, or at least in the period from July to October.

There are hundreds of farmers' markets to choose from, but you should probably stick with your local one. If you drive 200 miles to experience a new one, you are somewhat defeating the object.

7.

KAYAK DOWN AN AUTUMN RIVER, LOOKING AT THE CHANGING LEAVES

Leaf-viewing is one of the delights of autumn. In New England, the tourists who arrive for this purpose are called by the locals – perhaps in a spirit of mild derision – 'leaf-peepers', though the dollars they bring with them are presumably not unwelcome.

Possibly the best way of viewing autumn foliage is while floating down a river. As the paddle gently dips, the over-hanging trees glide past, an ever-changing Persian carpet of colour. The air is crisp, birds call from the forest, and there is the sweet scent of lea mould. Perhaps a deer or a fox comes down to d

If you don't fancy learning to operate a don't want an instructor tagging along, a punt for the day. Take along a pi

If it's just the two of you, and you're on an autumnal lover's break, you can't do better than some magnificent riverine location. It could take your relationship to a whole new level.

Also, there are only two directions to argue about.

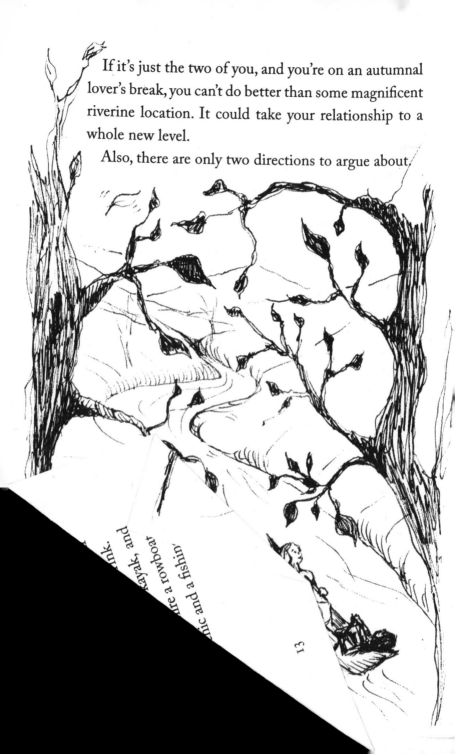

...nk.

...kayak, and

...re a rowboat

...nic and a fishin'

8.

GUZZLE OYSTERS

Thanks to modern aquaculture, oysters are in season all year round, but formerly they were harvested and eaten in the autumn months. The traditional advice was to eat oysters only if there was an 'r' in the month – September, October, November, and through to April – but not in the summer, when oysters would spoil. As a result, there are still many traditional oyster festivals in autumn. Among them are the Oyster Feast in Colchester, Essex, UK, in October, or the St. Michaels Oysterfest in Maryland, USA, in November. But perhaps the biggest and best-known of the current oyster extravaganzas is the oyster festival held in Hillsborough, County Down, Northern Ireland, in September.

The Hillsborough festival offers many delights. Among these are the Titanic Gala Ball, the Miss Oyster Pearl Beauty Competition and the Parade of

Nations. But what the crowds are really here to see is the Oyster Eating World Championships. This is part of the worldwide calendar of competitive eating (chicken wings, matzo balls, baked beans, pickles, hot dogs, jalapeno peppers, pizza, onions, cow brains, reindeer sausage, chocolate bars, quail eggs, crawfish, cabbage, corned beef hash, fritters, ice cream, mashed potatoes), in which grown men and women perform live in front of screaming crowds to shovel down as much of the specified food within a given time. In the oyster slurp-off, the world record was set by Colin Shirlow in 2005 with 233 oysters in three minutes, or 1.294 oysters per second: 4lbs of living meat, all packed away inside him and writhing over each other to avoid his digestive juices.

Disgusting? Certainly. But a strangely compelling spectacle.

9.

BE A WILDLIFE VOLUNTEER

There are plenty of reasons to get involved in wildlife conservation. You might wish to gain work experience, develop a hobby, get out of the house, take exercise, meet new people, or do something useful to protect the natural environment near where you live.

Work tends to be seasonal, but autumn is a good time for volunteering. There is a lot going on, chiefly repair and maintenance work before winter sets in. Common tasks include dry stone walling, woodland coppicing (cutting trees at ground level to encourage new growth), hide repair, tree pollarding (carried out on trees such as willows to maintain tree height and provide wood), bramble clearing, repair of stock fencing, hedge laying (creating and maintaining hedges), pond digging, scrub control, ditch management and path maintenance.

You can also get involved in monitoring and

surveying wildlife, for example, counting species in a given area, though some specialist knowledge may be required.

Or there may be opportunities near you to participate in growing schemes to provide food for a local area. You might get to take home food you've helped to grow.

Preparation? A packed lunch, some Wellington boots (preferably with steel toecaps), clothing suitable for the weather (waterproofs to be on the safe side), and a recent tetanus vaccination.

10.

SET OFF A FIRE LANTERN

In northern Thailand in November there is a Buddhist festival called Yi Peng. Originally the preserve of monks, it is a time for purging the past year's misdeeds and offering thanks and respect to the Buddha. Nowadays it has lost some of its monkish severity and has become a riotous popular carnival, the occasion for the release of a myriad of fire lanterns. These are paper constructions known as *khom loi* ('floating lanterns'), usually around a metre high, with a fuel cell underneath which fills the lantern with hot air. At a given signal hundreds are set alight to swarm upwards like fiery jellyfish; occasionally one of them catches fire and burns, trailing white-hot sparks. It is an extraordinary spectacle. The most famous Yi Peng celebrations are in Chiang Mai, where revellers not only set off lanterns but float lights on the river, set up spinning lights in doorways or temples and hold lanterns on sticks; there are also firework displays, parades of candle-lit floats, music and dancing.

Yi Peng is worth going halfway around the globe for, but if you can't afford the ticket, why not set off your own fire lanterns to celebrate autumn? 'Chinese lanterns' are cheap and easy to find. Buy a few dozen, go out to a piece of open ground with some friends and a few bottles of Thai Singha beer, and release them into the sky along with your wishes and dreams for the future.

Wait, if possible, for the correct date: the full moon in the second month of the ancient northern Thai Lanna calendar (usually around the end of November).

11.

FOLLOW THE RUT

The autumn rut is one of the most impressive spectacles of the natural world. The rut is the mating season, a build-up of testosterone-fuelled competition between male deer (stags) for access to females (hinds). During the rut, stags change physically: their antlers calcify and become harder, and they grow thick neck-manes. They also begin competitive roaring. A stag's roar sounds like something between a cow and a moped, with many belches, moans and backfires, signalling a challenge to other males. Pairs of stags can also be seen walking or running in parallel to size one another up, and when both refuse to yield, fighting ensues. These antler clashes are very much in earnest, and can result in severe facial or eye injuries, or even death through blood loss. As elsewhere among ruminants, the outcome is 'winner takes all'. Victorious stags build up the largest harems; the losers are sidelined, nursing their pride. Stags don't eat when they are in rut, and repeated challenges leave them drained and vulnerable. Possession of harems may therefore ebb and flow during the rutting season.

To see the rut, check with local wildlife groups. The National Trust in the UK can organise guided walks with a ranger and get you to the thick of the action. The deer are often so intent on each other that observers can get much closer than at other times of the year.

12.

SKETCH OUTDOORS

Autumn is a perfect time to sketch outdoors. Not too hot (no need for sunblock), not too cold (no need for gloves), and plenty of interesting natural scenes: trees in various stages of leaf, growing or harvested crops, stubble burning, fruit on the vine or tree, migrating skeins of geese, windfalls on the ground, drifts of leaves in the streets or fields.

You can sketch with a pencil on a pad, or pen and ink on cartridge paper, or with charcoal or pastels. You don't need all the paraphernalia of the painter: no easel, paintbox, palette or canvases. Just find a vantage point, sit on a rock or a shooting stick, and produce something quickly, without taking too much trouble or caring too much about the result. The fact that it's 'just' sketching has a remarkable effect; it frees you up to produce something spontaneous which will almost certainly be interesting to look at. Annotate the sketch, if you like, with comments about the colours or the weather, or indeed your feelings and ideas. This gives more interest to the finished product.

One tip: don't take an eraser with you. Allow for, and accept, your mistakes. Sketch in ink if possible, that way you know there's no going back, no polishing: sketch the moment, with all its fleetingness, making many drafts of a single scene. That way you will produce your freshest work.

13.

MAKE BILBERRY, WHORTLEBERRY, WHINBERRY, BLAEBERRY, FRAUGHAN OR BLACK HEART JAM

These are all the same fruit, most commonly known as the bilberry, found growing wild in temperate climates. Bilberries are small, round and purple with a white bloom to the skins. They have a dark red or purple interior with a finger-and-mouth-staining juice, and are *ipso facto* different from blueberries, which have a green interior. They can be used in pies, cakes, sorbets, liqueurs and ice cream, but their best-known use is in jam, where they give a flavour of unparalleled richness and density.

Making bilberry jam is simplicity itself. Just get a quantity of berries and remove stalks, leaves and insects. Put them in a pan with a cup of water and add two-thirds of their weight in sugar. A recipe of six cups of bilberries to four cups of sugar would do for a beginner. Crush the bilberries and bring to a boil. Keep boiling until the jam is of setting consistency. How to know this? Put a plate in the freezer, and when it is cold, spoon a little of the jam onto it. If, when you touch the jam, you notice it has a crinkly skin, this means the pectin in the fruit is working and will set the jam when it cools. (Since bilberries have a medium-to-low pectin content, using jam sugar or preserving sugar may help things along.)

Sterilise some jars and decant the jam into them. As long as the lids are tight and the jars are fully sterilised, your bilberry, whortleberry, whinberry, blaeberry, fraughan or black heart jam will keep for years.

14.

BOTANISE A WALNUT

A walnut is an extraordinary little package. Examining its constituent parts is a botanical adventure.

If you can, get a walnut directly from a tree. Walnuts grow encased in a fleshy green husk known as a pericarp, and the hard beige shell we are familiar with, known botanically as the endocarp, is inside, formed of two fused halves. Inside that is the intricately wrinkled brain-like formation of the walnut kernel, again in two fused halves called cotyledons, and separated from one another by a papery membrane. The kernel is covered by a thin brown skin known as the pellicle, or seed-coat, full of antioxidants (and able, incidentally, to induce powerful allergic reactions). The kernel, as well as being tasty, contains the ingredients for growing a new walnut tree: these include the radicle, or root, plus the plumule, or leaf-bearing shoot, both of which are activated by moisture to start the next generation.

Among all the nuts, there's something particularly fascinating about a walnut. Perhaps it's the walnut's sphericity, or the ease with which it can be broken down and reassembled, or the perfection of its complex and interlocking parts. In China today there is a craze for gambling on walnuts called *du he tao*: two walnuts, still in their green husks, are offered for sale to punters from a large batch, then opened and examined for symmetry. If the walnuts are similar enough, the punters can win large sums of money.

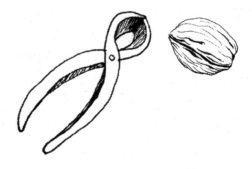

15.

GURN

To 'gurn' is to contort the face into bizarre and unlovely shapes. You might think that this is possible at any time of the year, but the World Gurning Championships take place as the leaves are beginning to turn: in mid-September, in a town called Egremont in Cumbria, England. The championships are part of the Egremont Crab Fair, which dates back to the 13th century. (In this case a 'crab' is not a crustacean, but a 'crab apple': see §71.) The Fair features a day of events, including 'climbing the greasy pole', but the undoubted highlight, capturing the most media attention, is the gurning.

The contestant who can look the ugliest – perhaps sticking out their lower jaw and bringing it up to cover their nose – wins. Winners are decided according to the volume of the shrieks of horror, despair and dismay. The gurner is required to make their gurn through a horse's braffin, or collar, and so the event is also called 'gurnin' through a braffin'.

Although it is a very rural, traditional event, anyone from around the world can enter. Those who can't attend personally may visit the Egremont Gurning website and upload a photo of themselves gurning, and may win the highly counter-cultural title of Unsymmetrical Face of the Month.

16.

ENJOY THE INDIAN SUMMER

This is the brief period between late September and early November when northern latitudes experience an unseasonable spell of warm weather. It seems to be a real phenomenon rather than merely a piece of wishful thinking, since all European languages have a term for it; and indeed it's also recognised in China, where it's called a 'tiger autumn'.

Why 'Indian'? The name is at least two centuries old and seems to date to the American colonial period. Some have suggested that it was the period when Native American raiding parties would use the excuse of good weather to mount attacks on European settlers ('it's very warm for the time of year, isn't it – fancy going and burning some log cabins?') but the theory seems to be largely discredited. A more probable origin is the derogatory use of 'Indian' to mean 'false', as in 'Indian giver' and

'Indian burn' (neither of which are supposedly 'real' or 'genuine').

With this in mind, the earlier English name for the same phenomenon, 'St Martin's Summer', is perhaps preferable. St Martin's Summer was named after St Martin's Day on November 11th, and an Indian Summer is called a St Martin's Summer in Italy (Estate di San Martino), Spain (Veranillo de San Martín), Portugal (Verão de São Martinho), and Wales (Haf Bach Mihangel).

In Eastern Europe (Lithuania, Hungary, Poland, Ukraine, Russia, and elsewhere) the term is 'Summer of old ladies'.

Which leads us on to …

17.

ACCEPT AGEING

Amid the plenty of autumn – the full granaries, the drowsy cider-scented breezes, the tins of baked beans in churches – there are constant reminders of decay. Leaves wither, insects die, fruit rots. To quote the Book of Common Prayer: 'In the midst of life we are in death.' Naturally in autumn, our thoughts turn to our own ageing and our own passage toward the grave.

As we all know, we live in a culture that values youth over age – one in which not only the policemen, but the gerontologists seem to be getting younger – and we all dread our birthdays after the age of 21. But fear of ageing is a terribly negative and destructive thing. It diminishes one's enjoyment of life and fosters feelings of inadequacy and exclusion. Accepting the fact that one is getting older can be a wonderful and liberating thing. Life is a daily gift, and no one, old or young, knows what tomorrow will bring: worrying about how old you are just sours the beauty of this gift. Ageing is really a privilege rather than a problem. In many parts of the world people die young, and never have the chance to be old. And even though age often also brings illness and sorrow, this is part of what it means to be human. Without the trials of life we would never have the chance to mature, never understand our parents and grandparents, and possibly never be truly happy.

According to surveys, in fact, the happiest age is 73.

18.

GO TO A LITERARY FESTIVAL

Every year there are hundreds of these around the world. You could go to three a week if you wanted to. At literary festivals there are many intriguing sights: fans stalking their favourite authors from reading to reading, as pumas do migrating deer; scrums of exhausted agents; business meetings of children's book publishers held at tiny plastic tables with plastic tea sets. Then there are theatrical performances, creative writing workshops, poetry readings, cookery demonstrations and the occasional parachuting-in of a bookish politician or Hollywood star. The festivals on offer are too numerous to list, but in the UK, the Cheltenham Literary Festival in October is one of the oldest and best attended. Others include the Folkestone and the Henley Literary Festivals in September; the Chester and the Peak Literary Festivals in October; and the Bridport Festival and

Dylan Thomas Festival (Swansea) in November. Outside the UK, September sees the Festivaletteratura in Mantua; the Brisbane Writers Festival; the Göteborg Book Fair in Gothenburg, Sweden; and the Winnipeg International Writers Festival. October sees the Singapore Writers Festival; Litquake in San Francisco; the Vancouver International Writers & Readers Festival; and the Khushwant Singh Litfest in Kasauli, India. November sees the Tanpinar Literature Festival in Istanbul; the Hong Kong Book Festival; the Guadalajara International Book Fair; and the Antigua and Barbuda International Literary Festival.

Autumn literary festivals, in short, are a book in themselves.

19.

MAKE SAPLINGS

Saplings are expensive in garden centres. With a little effort, you can grow your own.

Autumn is the best time to take cuttings from mature trees in your garden or neighbourhood. Wait until the last leaves have fallen; at this time the sap pressure is low, and you won't hurt the tree. (If you amputate branches in spring they can drip plaintively for weeks.) Now prune a section of the current year's new growth. Don't go beyond the new tip, which might be around a foot long; use a diagonal cut to maximise the surface area. If you can lay your hands on some hormone rooting powder, dust the cut, then pot the cutting up in some general purpose compost. When you've prepared a few of various species, put them outside for the winter. Hardwood cuttings (such as cherry, oak, birch, walnut, etc) need no additional heating or protection and can survive a frost, but if you have a greenhouse they might appreciate getting away from the wind. Roots will appear in spring, and the saplings will start to shoot up (they may need to be re-potted).

Now you can plant your saplings. Don't plant them in the wild, since natural ecosystems don't always need trees (marshlands, for example, are functioning ecosystems in their own right and trees would be an intrusion). But gardens are fine. Give your saplings away to your neighbours. Imagine being the progenitor of a hundred trees in a hundred gardens. That's quite a legacy, and it costs nothing.

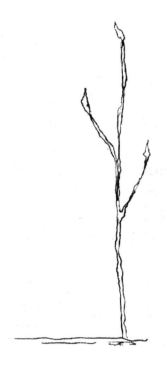

20.

USE YOUR EXTRA HOUR

In autumn, the clocks go strange. Our bodies know that it's time to get up, have breakfast, start the day's routine, but the clocks say that reality has been postponed and that we have an extra hour. The odd feeling persists throughout the day. Even at three o' clock in the afternoon it's very strange that it's not four. The children return from school in the dusk, slogging through black slimy leaves, and motorists put their lights on during rush hour.

If you plan ahead, you can have fun with your extra hour. How about something as simple as going out for a morning walk? You can pick sloes or rosehips, go cloud-spotting, or just saunter down to the end of the garden and see how your saplings are coming on.

Or you could do any of the following: write a real letter by hand to someone you have been neglecting; do an hour's concentrated thinking about where your life is going; meditate; memorise a poem; write a letter to your future self; plan a random act of generosity; invent a personal motto; send a message in a bottle; go for a bike ride; reflect on all the things you are grateful for and make a list, getting up to at least 30; write the first sentence of the novel you've been meaning to get around to; or look at your problems and ask yourself how many of them will be important five years from now.

Alternatively, roll over and go back to sleep.

21.

SCAN A FLY

As the weather gets colder, insects start dying. This is sad for them, but an opportunity for you. Using an ordinary optical scanner, you can create your own digitised insect collection, documenting the bugs in your locale.

Finding dead insects is not difficult. Houseflies, bumblebees and wasps batter themselves lifeless on the inside of windows; moths and butterflies, poetically ragged, can be found clinging in death onto garden bushes; dead ladybirds fall out of trees and land belly-up. Collect them and put them under the scanner.

You need to set for a reasonably high resolution, but it's surprising how well you can do even at low resolutions. A low file size can sometimes give just as much detail as a high file size. Experiment a little, zooming in and out, to see what results you get. A scanner will give you much better results than a cheap camera, enabling you to see fascinating details of an insect's head, mouth, even its individual hairs.

If you combine this with photos of things that are not scannable, you will be able to build up a collection of your backyard fauna without making a pin-hole in anyone's abdomen.

22.

WATCH A SCARY MOVIE

Horror films allow us to explore the shadowlands of our own fears. We see graphic, often sexualised, violence, raised to a pitch far higher than would be acceptable in other forms of entertainment, which allows us – perhaps much as the Roman arena did – to put our highly socialised selves aside for a couple of hours before returning to real lives in which problems can't be resolved by a swift machete-blow to the neck. Perhaps most importantly, horror films present us with death in a culture where death is not generally in plain view. Perhaps it is the sanitisation of death in normal life that makes horror films so essential.

The particular horror films that we choose may say something about us personally. If, for example, we are fans of *The Shining*, we may be secretly worried about writer's block; if *Hostel* is more our style, we may have concerns about Eastern European integration; and if

Invasion of the Bodysnatchers is our thrill of choice, we may be worried our garden is getting out of control.

Autumn is the horror film season par excellence. There is Halloween, of course (the holiday rather than the film), and the sense that the year is dying and that colder, grimmer times are coming, as well as the omnipresence of pumpkins, witches and alien cocoons (see §61). If any season is more horrifying than others, autumn is surely it.

23.

SEE *AUTUMN SONATA*

For an antidote to the above, although just as horrifying in its own way, watch *Autumn Sonata*, the 1979 film by Ingmar Bergman. A landmark in world cinema, it won a Golden Globe for best foreign language film, and starred Ingrid Bergman (no relation) in her final screen role, as well as the Ingmar Bergman stalwart Liv Ullmann.

The plot concerns a world-famous concert pianist, Charlotte (Ingrid Bergman) who, after the death of her long-term partner, decides to pay a visit to her daughter Eva (Liv Ullmann), who lives with her husband, a pastor, in a remote country parsonage. Charlotte has neglected Eva throughout her childhood, thinking only of her career, and in fact hasn't seen her for seven years. When Charlotte arrives she is surprised to discover that her second daughter Helena (Lena Nyman) is also living with

Eva: Charlotte long ago consigned Helena to a mental institution, but Eva rescued her and is looking after her. The tensions inherent in the relationship between mother and daughter build to a pitch where there is an emotional explosion, in which Eva tells her mother exactly she thinks of her and blames her for her own miserable life and relationships; Charlotte in her turn defends herself, explaining why she felt compelled to pursue her career at the expense of her family, making the picture more complex.

Loss, betrayal, death, mental illness, love, guilt and sorrow, a feast of Scandinavian gloom, set in a physical and metaphorical autumn.

24.

OBSERVE PUPATION

At the end of its life, a caterpillar fixes itself to the underside of a twig or leaf using a special glob of silk. It attaches itself to this glob using a special hook, then suspends itself from the hook and forms around itself a hard, protective shell. This is the pupa. In moths, the pupa is called a cocoon, in mosquitos it is called a tumbler, and in butterflies it is called a chrysalis.

Inside the shell astonishing changes begin to take place. The caterpillar acquires a whole new body plan, gaining wings, but also changing the number of its eyes and legs. Then, after a period typically of a couple of weeks, it secretes a liquid to dissolve the pupal case, or in some species rips the case apart using special claws. Wresting itself free, it pumps blood into its new wings to harden them. It then takes its place as a fully functioning adult, able to reproduce and watch 18-rated movies.

Butterfly chrysalises tend to be easiest to spot. You'll see them hanging from the undersides of twigs, perhaps looking a little like a dead leaf. (There is in fact a species of butterfly called the Autumn Leaf.) Carefully examine the shrubs and bushes in your locale. Butterflies often go through their life cycle several times a year, and in autumn will be doing so for the last time before hibernating for the winter.

Insects are very vulnerable during this time of inactivity, so some ingenious defences have evolved. In one species of butterfly, the pupa is guarded by ants inside their nest, the ants receiving a symbiotic benefit in the form of honeydew nectar.

25.

MAKE CHUTNEY

Chutney (from the Hindi word *chatni*) is a savoury relish served with meat, cheese, or in sandwiches. It's sometimes known as pickle. There's no real difference between chutney and pickle, although chutney may have a smoother texture.

Chutney doesn't really have a recipe. What goes in it is up to you. The usual candidates for chutney making are fruits, vegetables, sugar, spices and vinegar. Autumnal fruits and vegetables, windfalls, dried fruits and leftovers of various kinds are used. The permutations are effectively infinite. You can make prune chutney, chilli chutney, green tomato chutney, pear and fig chutney, peanut chutney, beetroot chutney, or walnut, coriander, banana, avocado and pineapple chutney (if you've a mind).

Once you've got the ingredients, chop the choppable things into small pieces (about fingernail size) and put

49

them in a pan with some vinegar, in a ratio of one part vinegar to six parts other ingredients. Cider vinegar or wine vinegar tastes better than ordinary fish-and-chip vinegar. Cover with water and simmer for a good hour until the ingredients have either dissolved or cooked very thoroughly. If you're using spices, place them in a muslin bag and then remove the bag at the end, otherwise your chutney will come out looking somewhat murky. Don't forget to include at least some sugar as it'll take the edge off the vinegar.

When the chutney is as thick as porridge and there is no water pooling at the top, it's ready. You can store it in glass jars, but don't use metal lids or the vinegar will corrode the metal.

26.

KNIT A SWEATER FOR WINTER

Knitting, to knitters, is both a physical and an intellectual activity, highly addictive and at the same time highly therapeutic, that provides a sense of connection with the past and a way of showing love for family and friends. And autumn is the ideal time to take it up. Come winter, you will need scarves, hats, sweaters, cardigans, gloves and balaclavas.

There's no space here to teach you to knit. The best way to start is probably to attend classes at a local adult education centre or get a good book on the subject. When you've learned a few basic skills (how to knit and purl, cast on, cast off and block), you can tackle your sweater. Beginners will almost certainly use a knitting pattern, which gives the complete instructions for making the garment in a particular size. Among variables that need to be considered are the gauge (number of stitches and rows per inch) of the garment, the weight of the yarn, its fibre content, its colour, and the needle size and type needed.

So, not a job for the faint-hearted, but a useful skill to learn for the autumn. And if you think knitting sounds rather pedestrian, you might like to bear in mind the words of one knitter, Stephanie Pearl McPhee: 'The number one reason knitters knit is because they are so smart that they need knitting to make boring things interesting. Knitters are so compellingly clever that they simply can't tolerate boredom.'

27.

CELEBRATE GUY FAWKES NIGHT

For centuries Guy Fawkes was the most reviled figure in British history. His crime is well known. On 5 November 1605 he and a group of Catholic conspirators attempted to blow up the House of Lords. They were discovered only moments before detonating their gunpowder; had it gone off, it would have killed King James I, who happened to be sitting in state at the time. Guy Fawkes betrayed his fellow plotters under torture, and they were rounded up and executed.

From that very first year, celebrations were held to celebrate the King's deliverance (it was later made an official holiday called Gunpowder Treason Day). Effigies of Guy Fawkes were burned, often alongside effigies of the Pope and the Devil. In one account from 1677 an effigy of the pope was filled with live cats 'who squalled most hideously as soon as they felt the fire'.

Historically, Guy Fawkes Night has also been the occasion for violent mayhem, often motivated by local politics. Rioting in Exeter in the 1860s and 70s, for example, led to the soldiery being called out, and in Guildford in the mid-nineteenth century, mischief-makers who called themselves 'guys' made sport with respectable householders, even perpetrating murder. Guy Fawkes Night was traditionally less about a good night out than about religion and politics, and tempers got frayed.

Nowadays, of course, Guy Fawkes Night (or Bonfire Night) is an occasion for family enjoyment and firework displays. The draining-away of any greater significance leads some to wonder however whether it will eventually be subsumed by two other autumn celebrations that fall almost on the same date: Halloween and Diwali.

28.

GO BONCO IN LEWES

One place where Guy Fawkes Night survives in earnest is Lewes in East Sussex. It is easily the largest Bonfire Night spectacle in the world, and draws an annual crowd of well over 80,000. Six bonfire societies parade through the town (overseen by the Bonfire Commission, or Bonco) towards their own firesites, where they set up rival fires. On the way, they carry flaming crosses to commemorate the seventeen Protestant martyrs from Lewes burned at the stake during the reign of Mary I (which actually preceded the attempted ignition of James I). Other events include flaming tar-barrel races (both men's and ladies') and Getting Very Drunk.

Lewes is possibly the only place in the country where you can see the anti-Catholic origins of Guy Fawkes Night in anything like their original vehemence. Effigies of the Pope are still regularly burned by the townspeople at the climax of the ceremonies, and some revellers march under anti-Papist slogans. Alongside the Pope are effigies of others who have attracted the marchers' ire in the previous year: these have included Osama bin Laden and local council leaders who opposed the celebrations.

So, not a place for anyone who values religious tolerance or being able to get into a pub without booking beforehand; but an astonishing continuation of the national and religious fervour of previous centuries in a largely secular culture.

29.

MAKE A GUY

This one is addressed to children. 'Penny for the Guy' seems to have disappeared from the cultural map during the last twenty years, and grown-ups, who have fond memories of making their own guys, feel nostalgic. So, kids, if you are reading this, get out there with a decently made guy (or even a reasonably acceptable one), and you will have to retreat from the hail of coins.

Here is a time-hallowed recipe for a quick and flammable Guy Fawkes. First of all get an old suit. You might find someone willing to give you one, or at a pinch you could get one from a charity shop (tell them it's for Guy Fawkes, and they may donate it out of sheer astonishment). Put an old T-shirt inside the jacket and stuff the chest and arms with rolled-up newspaper: do the same for the legs. Use a pair of old shoes for the feet and some gloves for the hands.

For the head, a pumpkin is fine (though heavy), but you can also use a pillow or a balloon. For the face, your job is slightly easier these days: you can use one of the masks made famous by anti-capitalist protesters from the film *V for Vendetta*. Give him a hat and some Jacobean locks if you can.

Put your guy in a wheelbarrow for easy transport and take him to the centre of town. Pose him in an interesting manner, perhaps holding a box of kitchen matches or with a sign that says: 'Unfortunately we cannot accept Visa'. You will make a *mint*.

30.

HAVE A BONFIRE

It could be a small bonfire of garden cuttings or a gigantic conflagration that will cause the paint on cars to blister at a distance of a hundred feet. It might be for Guy Fawkes Night, for Samhain, Hop-tu-Naa, Diwali, or just because you feel like having one. Whatever you choose, nothing says autumn better than a bonfire.

It's surprising how few adults know how to start a fire. The secret is really expressible in two words: surface area. You start with small stuff and then build up to bigger stuff. The smallest stuff is tinder. (Please refer to §101, 'Start a fire without matches.') Tinder can be a couple of sheets of newspaper balled up loosely, or some very thin dry twigs. On top of this, place kindling, which can be slender sticks of dry wood, about the size of pencils. On top of this, place thicker pieces of wood, and lots of them. And on top of them, logs.

A good, safe structure is to build up a fire with tinder and kindling, and then around it construct a square made with crosswise members, like a log cabin. This gives plenty of space for air-flow. A bonfire stacked like this should light from a single match and burn for hours without risk of collapse.

Choosing the right place is important. Be careful of overhead wires, trees or other vegetation that is at risk of being scorched, and nearby buildings. Have some buckets of water or a hose handy in case things don't go quite as planned.

One tip: it's difficult to start a fire using junk mail. No one knows why this is.

31.

SEE PONIES IN THE NEW FOREST

You can see ponies in the New Forest at any time of year, but the sight of these horses against the russet tones of the woodland is very beautiful indeed. New Forest ponies come in a variety of colours, but bay and chestnut – reddish-brown, to the uninitiated – are among the most common, giving them a resemblance to the turning leaves. New Forest ponies, one might say, are inherently autumnal.

Also in autumn the ponies are gathered up in 'drifts' for inspection. During these times, the ponies are given veterinary treatment and individually marked (their tails are shorn in a way that makes them recognisable as the wards of particular 'agisters' or forest administrators). Ponies in the New Forest are not strictly feral, but semi-feral.

Surprisingly perhaps, the vast majority of New Forest ponies – around four and a half thousand – are female. Stallions are kept in reserve and only released in small numbers – fifty or so – to do essential war work during the summer months. On these occasions each stallion collects a large number of mares as his personal harem and defends them against other stallions released at the same time. The foals born as a result are, if female, left with their single mothers, or if male, gelded or removed from the forest.

New Forest ponies can also be ridden, of course. A visit to the New Forest is a wonderful way to introduce children to riding, and the ponies are so sturdy and sure-footed that they can easily carry adults.

32.

GO ON A KEATS WALK

If you are fortunate enough to be in Winchester this autumn, you can go on the exact walk that Keats went on while living there and composing the famous poem *To Autumn*.

> Season of mists and mellow fruitfulness,
> Close bosom-friend of the maturing sun,
> Conspiring with him how to load and bless
> With fruit the vines that round the thatch-eves run …

The composition of the poem can be dated precisely to 19 September 1819, since Keats wrote about it to his friend John Hamilton Reynolds: 'Somehow a stubble plain looks warm – in the same way that some pictures look warm – this struck me so much in my Sunday's walk that I composed upon it.' Keats also obligingly set out the exact route of the walk in a letter to his brother and sister-in-law. It runs from his home near the Cathedral (resting place of Jane Austen), to the Inner Close, past Winchester College, through the water meadows, alongside the River Itchen, to the Hospital of St Cross ('a very interesting old place', as Keats succinctly described it), 'to St Cross meadows till you come to the most beautifully clear river'. The letter is also dated in the week of 19 September 1819.

Alternatively you can do without Winchester, and simply visit any beautiful wild place in autumn. After all, the poem, a great meditation on the beauty and plenitude, but also the moribundity, of the natural world, exists untrammelled by Winchester.

> Where are the songs of Spring? Ay, where are they?
> Think not of them, thou hast thy music too.

33.

DATE A HEDGE

We're not talking garden hedges here, but agricultural hedges (or hedgerows). Farmers have always separated off their land from neighbouring plots to mark boundaries ('good hedges make good neighbours'), or to prevent animals straying. Hedges provide a link with the past that few other things in the landscape can offer. Often unremarkable stretches of hedge can prove to be many hundreds, even thousands of years old.

The simplest way to date a hedge is to count the plant species present in a given stretch. Very roughly, the more species, the older it is. The usual method is to take a 30m stretch of hedge and apply the formula:

x (age) = y (number of species) x 110 + 30.

So, if you find six species, the hedge is 690 years old, putting it at around the early 13th century. This would be a perfect finding, in fact, since many live hedges were created in this period under legislation by kings John and Richard, who allowed the sale of royal woodland for agricultural land, as long as the land was adequately hedged to prevent incursions by the royal deer.

There are many complications to dating hedges – and it's possible to be wildly out, due, for instance, to the fact that many modern hedges are deliberately planted to allow for maximum biodiversity – but with attention to particular indicator species (such as hawthorn) and other factors such as the presence or absence of trees, you can become more expert. And to cheat, you can cross-check your results against local historical records and maps.

34.

LOOK FOR CLIMATE CHANGE BY FILLING OUT A NATURAL CALENDAR

The majority of scientists say that climate change is real. But how do we, the non-specialists, really know? Climatology is a subject outside the purview of non-specialists. However, by observing the natural world for ourselves we can at least go part of the way to having an informed opinion.

Filling out a nature calendar this autumn – a record of the seasonal indicators as they happen year on year – helps to take some of the responsibility back and have something to contribute to the discussion.

For example, the fly agaric. In my part of Norfolk, this mushroom makes its appearance in mid-September, but it seems to be getting later. Have a look yourself and record the data. What about other plants and animals? For example, what time do house martins and swallows depart, and redwings and fieldfares arrive? Make entries for shrubs such as elder, blackthorn, holly, hawthorn, dog rose, bramble and hazel. When do they first get their full autumn tinting? When do the leaves begin to fall? And when is the shrub bare? Have a look at trees such as ash, maple, oak, beech, horse chestnut and sycamore. What are they doing? Record diseases such as the leaf miner moth in horse chestnut. Even the time when you last cut your lawn as you get ready for winter could be a significant entry in your nature calendar.

Nature calendar templates can be downloaded from the Woodland Trust and other organisations.

35.

GO MOTHING

It's an autumn evening, dry and pleasantly chilly, and you are out in the school playing fields with your light box as the last glimmers of the waning sun tint the clouds. You are mothing.

You can do this in your garden or out in the wilds. The simplest trap consists of a light source and a box where the moths can collect. Mercury vapour lamps are the best source of illumination, but ordinary bulbs will do the job pretty well. Various lures can be used: pheremone-based scents are good for some species, whereas others respond well to sugary water (simulating nectar).

When you have collected a good supply, it's time to identify them. There are dozens of families of moths, and tens of thousands of species, so you will need a good field guide. Moths, though colourless, have colourful names. They include the Reed Leopard, the

Apple Leaf Skeletoniser, the Cotoneaster Webworm, the Beautiful China-mark, the Large Tabby, the Drinker, the Dwarf Cream Wave, the Many-lined, the Geometrician, the Three-humped Prominent, the Ni Moth, the Shark, the Buff Footman, the Setaceous Hebrew Character, the Pale Stigma and the L-Album Wainscot.

A moth-trapper is called a mother, but this is sometimes ambiguous if written down.

36.

IDENTIFY THE SIX BUTTERFLY FAMILIES

Unlike moths, which exist worldwide in dozens of families, there are only six major families of butterfly. These are the swallowtails, the gossamer-wings, the brushfoots, the metalmarks, the skippers, and the whites and sulphurs. Learning to tell them apart is an easy way to get started in lepidoptery.

Swallowtails, first of all, can be recognised by the decorative adjuncts to their hindwings, sometimes in the form of scalloped appendages. Swallowtails tend to be medium-to-large in size (the biggest butterflies in the world are swallowtails) and are brightly patterned. Gossamer-wings are smaller and get their name from the reflectivity and silky smoothness of their wings: they are divided into blues, coppers, harvesters and hairstreaks. Brushfoots are distinguished by the fact that they seem only to have four legs: in fact they have six like other insects, but the front legs are much shorter and are sometimes difficult to see. Metalmarks are so-called because of their metallic spots. Skippers tend to have stubby wings and thick bodies. Whites and sulphurs are either white or yellow, usually with small black markings: the cabbage white is the most familiar representative.

Butterfly collecting and butterfly identification are a lifetime's work that can become an obsession. The lepidopterist and author of *Lolita* Vladimir Nabokov said: 'If my first glance of the morning was for the sun, my first thought was for the butterflies it would engender.'

See also §24, 'Observe pupation'.

37.

OBSERVE MIGRATING LEPIDOPTERA

Or you can specifically look for migratory butterflies and moths. This is difficult for the amateur, but with a good field guide and the right location it is not impossible.

Migration is common throughout the animal kingdom. Seals, whales, and fish do it; so do sheep, deer, and caribou. And so do butterflies and moths. As with other animals, it's an attempt to gain an advantage through an expansion of their feeding or breeding range.

The most famous butterfly migration is probably that of the Monarch butterfly, which flutters gamely every year from Canada to Mexico: similar migrations take place across the globe, on every continent except Antarctica. In Europe, numerous species fly north in the warm weather and then back south again as conditions cool. Recent studies have shown an increase in the numbers of migratory species reaching the south of England: in a long-term study carried out between 1982 and 2005, seventy-five migratory lepidoptera species were logged at a single location on the south coast of England, increasing at a rate of about 1.5 new species per year. Each butterfly or moth had to traverse a minimum of 93 miles (150km) of open water to reach the site. Species recorded included the Pearly Underwing, the Small Mottled Yellow, the Hoary Footman, the Bedstraw Hawk, the Old World Webworm, and Radford's Flame Shoulder.

38.

TRAIN YOUR MEMORY

If you're having difficulty distinguishing one butterfly from another, you may wish to hone your memory skills.

There are many ways of doing this, but one way might be to enter the World Memory Championships, held at various locations around the globe (London, Guangzhou, Kuala Lumpur, Bahrain) in the autumn months. Heats and local competitions are also held throughout the year. The Championships were founded in 1991 by the inventor of mind-mapping, Tony Buzan, and the chess grandmaster, Raymond Keene. The most famous memoriser thrown up by the championships is probably the first world title-holder, Dominic O'Brien, who was often seen on television memorising packs of playing cards.

Events in the championships include Spoken Numbers, Playing Cards, Historic/Future Dates,

Binary Numbers, Abstract Images, Names and Faces, Random Numbers, Speed Numbers, Speed Cards and Random Words (oxygen, lovely, temporise, stepfather, buttock, smashing, timeshare).

Whether you decide to enter the championships or not, memory training can benefit your studies and your working life, and it's available to all, whether you've been born with a great memory or not. Memory, it seems, is a faculty that expands the more you use it. To quote founder Tony Buzan: 'Memory is a lost art. These days we rely on our phone, iPads and computers to memorise things on our behalf, and as a result we are not exercising our most important muscle: our brains.'

39.

LIE YOUR HEAD OFF

If you can't remember things, tell lies instead. You may even win a prize. The World's Biggest Liar competition, an autumnal festival of fibs, is held every year in November at the Bridge Inn, Santon Bridge, Cumbria.

It all began in 1974, when the title of 'World Champion Liar' was bestowed on Will Ritson, the landlord of the Wasdale Head Inn in Victorian times, who claimed to have bred a cross between an eagle and a foxhound which was capable of jumping over houses. Later winners included a Cretan who claimed that all Cretans were liars and a bishop who claimed simply 'I have never told a lie' (though these stories may be apocryphal).

The present contest has now been running nearly forty years, and the supply of talent seems to be inexhaustible. Competitors are not exclusively British:

entrants hail from around the world, and the first international winner was Abrie Krueger from South Africa in 2003. Other winners have included the comedian Sue Perkins, who won the competition in 2006 with a story about the eructations of sheep causing a hole in the ozone layer. So far none of the local estate agents have put in an appearance. Each entrant is allowed between two and five minutes, and may tell their tall tales in Cumbrian dialect. The secret to successful lying, the event's organisers claim, is to hover near the truth without actually alighting on it.

Oh, and the prize is a million pounds. Honest.

40.

TAKE AUTUMN PHOTOS

The light is different in autumn. The sun is lower in the sky and hits the horizon at a different angle; often it will filter through trees, taking on their autumnal gold or red tones, and, as the trees thin, more light strikes the ground, throwing long shadows. The light is softer, hazier, less intense, more lateral. It is excellent for photography, because direct sunlight doesn't necessarily help bring out colour, and in fact more often bleaches it, merging colours together. A diffuse light, perhaps on a cloudy day, is best for taking pictures, allowing colours to glow with their full richness. What the eye may see quite dully, the camera picks up and intensifies.

There is so much colour in autumn that is not available in any other season. The leaves are every conceivable hue from green to puce, to purple and black, and look extraordinary against the changing autumn skies. Trees and woods work particularly well in compositions where foliage is reflected in water.

Try to ring the changes on some of the stock images of autumn photography. Try getting down low so you can shoot through mushrooms or fallen leaves; try actually capturing the dance of leaves as they whirl in a vortex in a busy street; or attempt to get to grips with some of the decay of autumn – dead animals, rotten fruit, discarded cider-pressings, abandoned summer toys.

41.

WATCH ANIMALS PREPARING TO HIBERNATE

Did you know that snails hibernate? They do. They seal up their shells and go into suspended animation for months on end. A wide variety of other animals also exhibit hibernating behaviour: they include bats, dormice, adders, grass snakes, toads, bumblebees, wasps and ladybirds.

Let's pick one species: the hedgehog. This will begin preparing for hibernation around September. First of all, it needs to put on fat, and may build up its fat reserves to around 30% of its entire body weight before it retires for the winter. Expect hedgehogs to be much more active, therefore, in the autumn, but don't approach them if you encounter them. A hedgehog in frantic search of insects or worms won't take your intrusion kindly and may bite.

From November onwards, a hedgehog will prepare its hibernaculum in piles of leaves or wood. If you have a heap of raked leaves in your back garden, therefore, think twice before jumping into it in Wellington boots. If you are planning a bonfire, check your wood-pile first.

The hedgehog then goes into a deep sleep, lowering its metabolism and body temperature and drawing all heat into the core of its body. Temperature goes down from 35°C to 10°C, and heart-rate is lowered from 190 per minute to a zombie-esque 20. Blood flow to the brain drops, sending it into a self-induced coma. It is vulnerable to predators at this time, but fortunately instinctive defences can cause it to bristle its spines at any disturbance.

Hibernation is one of nature's quieter but most fascinating spectacles, and late autumn offers the opportunity to see it in action.

42.

FEED THE BIRDS (TUPPENCE A BAG)

In the autumn, birds such as the redwing, fieldfare, waxwing and brambling arrive from colder climes such as Scandinavia and Russia. Simultaneously, birds such as the swallow, house martin and chiffchaff depart for Africa.

These migratory birds – plus our domestic blackbirds, bullfinches and sparrows – are all in need of a good feed in autumn. They need a feed all year round, of course, but in autumn they are renewing their feathers – the autumn moult – which takes energy.

You can feed the birds a wide range of foods, including seeds, grains, nuts, fat, fruit and rice. You can even feed them the sort of thing they would be eating in the wild: insects or grubs. You can get these from a fishing supply shop, though make sure the insects are dead first or they'll mount an escape from the bird table. Pre-loaded feeders often use fat or suet, and for good reason. This provides birds with the greatest energy and attracts the broadest range of bird species.

You can also supply birds with water. A bird drinker is better than a bowl because there is a reduced chance that the birds will foul the water. In fact, if you have a feeding station, be prepared to clean it regularly, or you may be doing more harm than good. Birds transmit diseases to one another, and a dirty feeding station is like a slum tenement for humans.

And while they're feeding outside your window, you have the pleasure of observing them. (Birds *can* see you through glass, but they know you can't touch them through it.)

43.

MARK THE DAY OF THE DEAD

No, not the zombie film directed by George Romero. The day, either November 1st or 2nd, corresponding to All Saints' Day and All Souls' Day in the Catholic calendar, on which people celebrate the lives of their deceased relatives.

The Day of the Dead is most associated with Mexico, where it is a public holiday, but it is observed throughout Latin America, as well as in the USA, Europe and elsewhere. The celebrations involve many things, and differ from place to place, but will often include visits to graves and cemeteries to lay flowers (particularly marigolds); the setting up of shrines, in houses or in the street, featuring pictures of the departed or mementoes of their lives and loves; the offering of food and drink to departed souls (which can then be consumed after the souls have taken the spiritual essence of the offerings); and parades and parties. The Day of the Dead has a Christian flavour, but aspects of it can be traced back to Aztec festivities. People dress as skeletons or devils, and there is a spirit of mild mayhem abroad which extends to the playing of practical jokes.

In Mexico, amateur poets create verses called 'calaveras' (or 'skulls') to satirise their dead relatives or mock the living. If you want to mark the Day of the Dead, why not write one? Here's an example to get you started:

> Marcialita the housekeeper
> Expended so much lack of energy
> That by not doing anything
> She turned into a *calavera*.

44.

DECORATE WITH AUTUMN LEAVES

Many cultures celebrate the turning of autumn leaves: New England is justly celebrated as a world centre of leaf beauty, and the Japanese greet the fierce autumn leaves of Hokkaido with almost as much fervour as they greet the blossom of the plum or cherry (see §46, 'Eat autumn leaves').

It's tempting to bring that beauty into the house, even if only briefly, and there are various ways you can create an attractive display with leaves and other autumnal plant materials (nuts, cones, berries, twigs, needles).

One method you might like to try is a simple autumn table display. Get some twigs with the leaves still attached (snip them off, if it's your tree) and arrange them in a vase. For an interesting effect, add leaves you have made yourself out of gold or red paper, or perhaps out of pages cut from magazines; affix these at points where real leaves would grow. Scatter leaves around the base of the display.

Or try creating bookends made out of leaves in glass jars. The leaves will last for a long time, though not forever: you can do your best to preserve them by ironing them between wax paper to dry them out (it's the moisture that makes them rot).

There are plenty of other ways to use autumn leaves. You can create strings of leaves to cover a wall; create a beaded curtain with leaves instead of beads; or experiment with leaf mobile designs. Leaves are the ultimate craft material, and they're entirely free of charge.

45.

COMPOST LEAVES

Many people burn leaves at the end of autumn, but it's not the most pleasant way to dispose of them. A bonfire is one thing, but a leaf-fire that gives no warmth and smothers the neighbourhood in a yellow fog for hours is another. There's a much greener alternative: make them into leaf mould.

You can do this in one of two ways, depending on how many leaves you have to process. The first is simply to put them in black plastic bags. Puncture the bags at the bottom and load the leaves in. Tie them off at the top and wait for a year. The leaves will have magically broken down into moist, friable leaf-mould.

If you have a lot of leaves to deal with and don't want plastic bags filling your garden, you can make a simple leaf-locker. This is a very basic holder made of chicken wire. Try the following design: get some treated wooden stakes and bang them into the ground to form a rectangle one metre wide by one-and-a-half metres long. Wrap chicken wire around the stakes to form an enclosure. Don't make it too high because you're going to need to get in there with a fork later to get the leaf mould out. Fill it with leaves and wait. You may wish to protect the top by a loose tarpaulin tied at the corners.

Leaf mould is useful in the garden in a variety of ways. Leaves are full of nutrients and minerals, and can be added to poor soils. You can use them as a top-dressing around the roots of plants, or as a mulch, preventing weeds from growing and stopping evaporation.

Alternatively you can go greenest of all and eat your leaves (see the next section).

46.

EAT AUTUMN LEAVES

Yes, that's right, eat them. No longer do you have to be content merely with observing them, composting them, decorating with them or throwing them in the air. It's a Japanese custom, and it's called *momiji tempura*, or maple leaves in batter. There can be few better ways of really connecting with the season, deep down inside.

Tempura is the Japanese art of frying in crispy, highly textured batter, and the usual victims are prawns, squid and vegetables, though if you go to Japan it's also possible to see tempura-fried fruit, sweet dumplings or ice cream (the Japanese answer to Baked Alaska). For *momiji*, the leaves themselves are quite small – the Japanese maple is cuter than the Canadian – so after frying they come out rather like maple-shaped potato crisps. The shape is the point, really, because the leaves themselves don't taste of much. The batter can be flavoured with different ingredients, including sugar and soy sauce, and the finished result may be dusted with sesame seeds.

Aficionados say that the sound of eating *momiji tempura* – a gentle munching – is similar to the sound of walking through a fall of leaves dried by the mild autumn sunshine.

You can make your own *momiji* with maple, but it's probably best to hold off on other species of tree until toxicological tests have been conducted.

47.

GO LAWN MOWER RACING

The sport sputtered into life in the early 1970s, fuelled by dissatisfaction at the high cost of motor sport. It was immediately popular, and was given a boost by the enthusiasm of Oliver Reed and Stirling Moss, the latter of whom won the British Grand Prix for lawn mowers in 1975 and again in 1976 (now I call that greedy).

There are four classes: petrol mowers driven by a roller that you run behind; roller-driven mowers with towed seats; small wheel-driven mowers with rear engines; and garden tractors with an engine in front. The rules are: mowers must have been originally designed and sold to mow domestic lawns, and cannot be modified (except to remove the blades for safety); there must be no sponsorship; there are no cash prizes; and any revenue raised goes to charity. Lawn mower racing is thus a rather refreshing antithesis to motor sport in general.

Heats are held throughout the year, but the long shadows and lush greenery of autumn, and its association with hazy days spent in the garden or tending the cricket pitch, makes it the ideal time to join in. In fact, you don't have to live in the UK to participate: championships are also held in the USA, Canada, Australia, New Zealand and elsewhere.

In search of a motto for the proceedings, the organisers first came up with 'Sic biscuitis disintegrat', or 'that's the way the cookie crumbles', but thought better of it and settled on 'Per herbam ad astra', or 'from the grass to the stars' (with a nod to the Royal Air Force). This was held to invoke 'everything spiritual in lawns'.

48.

HAVE AN AUTUMN DECLUTTER

Autumn is a good time to reorganise your living space. The days are cooler and you can work up a sweat lugging boxes and bags to the dump or to the charity shop. It's rather like making your nest ready for winter: a place for everything, and everything in its place. And no junk.

There is a law that states that 70% of your possessions are only used 1% of the time, with the remaining 20% used 5% of the time and only the top 10% used 50% of the time. This is a difficult law to remember (or apply), but what it boils down to is that everyone has at least one roll of grimy carpet, a swingball set, some mouldering abstract canvases in acrylic, an experimental barbecue, five cans of solid paint, twenty-five model dinosaurs, two tins of red boot polish, some bolts, three airline sick bags and a tote bag full of out-of-date medicines. These must be donated to someone who needs them, or to landfill, immediately. After all, if you don't get rid of them there won't be room for the new junk you will soon acquire.

Autumn is also a good time for a bonfire (see §30) of all the paperwork, old course notes, bills (paid), and bits of miscellaneous cardboard that you thought might come in useful around 1985. Most satisfying of all you can burn your old journals and diaries, or your Great Undiscovered Literary Works. Burn them! You'll feel ever so much better afterwards.

49.

CELEBRATE HOP-TU-NAA

Hop-tu-Naa! Put in the pot
Hop-tu-Naa! Put in the pan
Hop-tu-Naa! I burnt me throat
Hop-tu-Naa! Guess where I ran?

Hop-tu-Naa is a version of Halloween that originates from the Isle of Man. Celebrated on the 31st of October, it marks the changing of the year and the moment when the gathering forces of winter begin to take hold: it's also a time when Manx spirits abound and when ghostly Manx stories are told. As in other Halloween traditions, there is an emphasis on the marriage of girls. Games are played in which girls try to see their future husbands using various methods of divination, such as the making of Soddag Valloo or Dumb Cake. After this very salty and probably rather nasty cake (it's got eggshells in it) has been eaten, the girls who have partaken go to bed and hope they will dream of a future husband offering them a glass of water.

The origin of the word 'Hop-tu-Naa' is uncertain, but its similarity to 'Hogmanay', the Scottish new year, suggests that the two have a common root; and some of the ancient traditions of Hop-tu-Naa later migrated to the Manx New Year. In Hop-tu-Naa, as in Hogmanay, there is a preoccupation with coal. Coal dust is smeared on the hearth and if a footprint appears overnight, it can presage either a birth or a death, depending on whether it points in or out.

> Hop-tu-Naa! I ran to the well
> Hop-tu-Naa! And drank my fill
> Hop-tu-Naa! And on the way back
> Hop-tu-Naa! I met a witch cat
> Hop-tu-Naa!

50.

MAKE AN AUTUMN WREATH

Christmas wreaths are a familiar sight in winter. They're usually crafted from evergreen plants such as holly and ivy. But there is a long tradition of autumn wreaths too. These celebrate autumn colours and the changing of the seasons, and can be used for exterior decoration, for example on a door, or inside a house as a table setting or on a wall. They're also fun to make.

To get started you need a circular frame of some kind, perhaps made from wire or twisted plant fibres. You can buy these or make your own. A simple way to make a frame is to use a wire coat hanger, which has a ready-made hook at the top for hanging the wreath up; just bend the triangular hanger into a circle. Now you need to choose some materials. Leaves, most obviously: try to find leaves with long stems, such as sycamore, plane or maple, which will help you attach them. There are many other materials that you can use: pine cones, bark, nuts, berries and twigs are all beautiful (just don't despoil trees or moss banks to get them). Now you need to fix your materials to the frame. Tying with thread is one option, though it may be a bit fiddly. As soon as you've got a few tied on, you'll be able to weave other stems in without further tying. Another option is to use a hot glue gun to attach each piece. Cover the frame thickly, making sure none of the wire is showing. Et voila! An autumn welcome to your visitors.

If you want to make a Halloween wreath, add some models of witches or skulls.

51.

READ SOME POEMS ADDRESSED TO THE SEASON

There is a rich vein of English poetry taking autumn as its theme. The reason is not difficult to guess. After the orgies of spring and summer, in autumn we are forced to acknowledge that there is a price to be paid. We are still surrounded by plenty and by riches, to be sure – we may even be enjoying an Indian Summer – but things are already beginning to wither and decay. The application to our own lives is inescapable: we too must finally wane (or as Rossetti puts it, 'Know'st thou not at the fall of the leaf/How the soul feels like a dried sheaf/Bound up at length for harvesting,/And how death seems a comely thing/In Autumn at the fall of the leaf?'). This gives autumnal writing a uniquely multilayered character.

A good starting point might be John Keats' poem *To*

Autumn (see §32). Next you might try the wonderful *Spring and Fall* by Gerard Manley Hopkins. Also have a look at the following: *To Autumn* by William Blake, *Autumn* by John Clare, *Come Up from the Fields, Father* by Walt Whitman, *The Wild Swans at Coole* by William Butler Yeats, *Blackberrying* by Sylvia Plath, *Autumn* by Siegfried Sassoon, *September Midnight* by Sarah Teasdale, *Nothing Gold Can Stay* by Robert Frost, *Autumn Song* by Dante Gabriel Rossetti, *Brink of Death* by Nakahara Chuya, *Autumn* by Amy Lowell, *At Needlehole* by Alison Brackenbury, *Geese* by Michael Shorb and *Song-Day in Autumn* by DH Lawrence.

52.

MAKE LEAF JEWELLERY

There are various ways to make jewellery out of leaves, but two of the most effective and simple are resin dipping and clay modelling.

In the first method, you use resin to coat the leaf. First of all, gather some leaves appropriate for a pendant, necklace, or earrings. Smaller leaves are usually better. Press each leaf between the pages of a book until thoroughly dry. Then dip into or brush with resin. Resins can be bought from craft stores and will often come as a two-part kit (catalyst plus resin). When the resin is dry, drill holes in the leaf for attachment to a chain or earring hook.

The second method involves using the leaf to make an impression in clay. For this you will need some polymer clay that can be fired at low temperatures in a domestic oven: alternatively you can use air-hardening clay that works with a catalyst. This second type of clay gives you about a 15-minute window to shape your leaf, which is usually enough. Roll the clay out thinly (about as thin as a coin) and impress the leaf into it. Now, leaving the leaf in place, cut around the edges. Unpeel the leaf to reveal the veining, then shape the leaf if desired (bend the edges round slightly to give it a more natural look) and either oven-bake or leave to harden. When it's ready, paint the clay – metallic colours work well. Drill holes for fixings as above.

You now have a permanent reminder of the beauty of autumn.

53.

CRAFT AN APPLE DOLL

Apple dolls are a North American folk art. Only the heads of the dolls are made from apples, the rest of the body, usually with clothing reminiscent of the eighteenth and nineteenth centuries, is made from non-apple materials.

To make an apple doll, follow these steps. First of all, select a large, fresh, sound apple. Peel it carefully. Carve it into a head. The part of the face that sticks out most is the nose, so reserve an area for the nose, and carve away material to produce the eyes, cheeks and mouth. When you're satisfied with the result, place the carved apple into a small bath of water and lemon juice (use a couple of teaspoons of lemon juice) for ten minutes or so, to prevent browning. Now leave it to dry. This will take a long time in ordinary household conditions, and if the temperature is not high enough, the apple will rot instead of drying. You can use an oven, but make sure the temperature is very low, or the apple will turn to apple sauce.

Your apple is dry when it is spongy to the touch. Now add some beads for eyes, and use paint to create accents on the head, particularly around the eyes, cheeks and mouth. Add wool for hair. Put a wire through the base of the head and fasten it to a wire skeleton. Pad out the skeleton and make some clothes. Your apple doll is complete.

Because apples wizen when they dry, apple dolls all look like ancient crones and codgers, and are rather creepy. But they are quite a talking point.

54.

RING BIRDS

Birds can be ringed (not rung) at any time of the year, but autumn is a signal for change in northern latitudes as some birds arrive from colder climes and their less-hardy cousins leave for the south. The affixing of small bands of aluminium or plastic to birds' legs (and sometimes their necks or wing-feathers) helps ornithologists keep track of them all. The ring contains the bird's vital statistics as an individual, and if the bird is later re-trapped, the data can be compared to their current status. In this way it's possible to see, for example, how old a bird is, or how far it has migrated (the most frequent-flyer miles clocked up by any bird is the tiny Arctic tern at around 44,000 miles/71,000 km per year).

Ringing doesn't hurt birds, and is not known to impede their behaviour in any way: if it did, then it would defeat its purpose. But you can't just get out there and do it yourself. Training is necessary. Fortunately there are many ringing centres throughout the world, and in ornithophiliac countries such as the UK and USA, it's easy to find a trainer. No prior knowledge is necessary, though if you have an interest in birds and can tell the difference between a finch and a tit on a frosty autumn morning you will have an advantage. After training, which can take up to a year, you get a permit, which means you can go ringing on your own.

Ringing has established the age of the oldest recorded bird in the world, an albatross called Wisdom, who was first ringed in 1956, and in 2013 was 62 years old. In that year she raised a healthy chick.

55.

MAKE A LAVENDER POTPOURRI

Potpourri, of course, is a concoction of flowers, oils and other ingredients, designed to produce a pleasant aroma in a room. Potpourri means 'rotten pot' in French, which isn't immediately appealing. The name refers to the fact that wet or macerated ingredients were traditionally used to make potpourri, though nowadays it is perhaps more popular to make the dry kind.

Flowers which bloom in spring or summer can be plucked and left to dry in a warm, dark place with a good circulation of air. They will then be ready for use by the autumn months. Lavender is an excellent choice as a base for your potpourri, but you can also use roses, carnations, or any other aromatic flower.

To make a simple dry potpourri, take about three cupfuls of dried flower heads, and add to this two tablespoons of chopped orris root. The orris root acts as a fixative: it absorbs the fragrance and makes the potpourri aromatic for much longer. If you can't find any orris root, other fixatives include tonka bean or calamus root – you can even use dried woodchips. Now add some essential oils. The fragrance of the lavender and other flowers won't provide enough scent on their own, so experiment with oils such as geranium, lemon, bergamot, patchouli or ylang ylang. To this you can add herbs, mint, lemon balm or other notes as your fancy beckons. Experiment a little.

Leave this mixture for two weeks in a sealed container to develop a scent. Then put it into jars, sachets or bags for display around the house. A very nice addition to your home – or even a Christmas gift (see §76).

56.

DISCOVER ANCIENT TREES

The longest-lived entities in the natural world are trees. The oldest of all individual trees are the bristlecone pines, specimens of which have been dated at 5,000 years old: they would have germinated at roughly the time when humans were inventing writing. Trees that propagate as clones of one another, such as the quaking aspen, can live even longer. One such colony of trees is Pando (Latin for 'I spread') in the Fishlake National Forest in Utah. This tree, which looks like several trees, is actually a single super-organism connected by a root system, and is probably around 80,000 years old. As well as being the oldest, it's also the heaviest known life form on earth.

Britain and Europe are well served for ancient trees. The Llangernyw Yew is the oldest tree in Europe, and can be visited in the churchyard of the village of Llangernyw in North Wales. It's almost as old as a bristlecone pine, at somewhere between 4,000 and 5,000 years old. Other ancient or veteran trees, many thousands of years old, are common throughout the countryside. Since they tend to be larger, they support a greater number of living things in their branches and root systems. They also give us a link to our own history and to the Wild Wood that covered Europe before humans cleared the forests. They are part of our folklore (Hansel and Gretel, Hoods Robin and Red Riding) and collective memory.

They are also very vulnerable to development, damage and disease. To cherish ancient trees is to protect an important aspect of our heritage.

57.

CELEBRATE APPLE DAY

The first Apple Day was on 31 October 1990, and was held at London's Covent Garden. It was organised by the group Common Ground, whose aim is to celebrate the diversity of the British landscape and its varied farming produce. On that first Apple Day there were 40 stalls featuring traditionally made ciders and juices, apple chutneys, jellies, pies and puddings; there were displays by apple-jugglers and apple-inspired writers and musicians; there were longest-peel contests and demonstrations by apple blossom beekeepers. It was such a success that the idea spread country-wide, and Apple Day is now held annually in October at village halls, museums, farmers' markets and local history societies. Currently there are many hundreds of events per year, and the idea has spread overseas. The day taps into our sense of the beauty of apples and orchards, and gives a forum to those who value regional foods.

The most common event found at Apple Days is probably simple apple identification. Since that first experiment in the Garden of Eden, thousands of apple varieties have been created by patient grafters and pruners, very few of which ever get into a supermarket. Ask at your local hypermart for a Bloody Ploughman, a Winterton Cod or a Veronica's Honeydew and you'll get short shrift. Many of these apples are just too big, too knobbly or too flavourful for them to take a risk. To see these apples lined up on trestle tables, to hear about their histories, and then to buy them and sink your teeth into them is a unique pleasure.

58.

PICK APPLES

> My instep arch not only keeps the ache,
> It keeps the pressure of a ladder-round.
> I feel the ladder sway as the boughs bend.
> And I keep hearing from the cellar bin
> The rumbling sound
> Of load on load of apples coming in.
> – Robert Frost, *After Apple-Picking*

Robert Frost had to ascend a ladder, its two forks pointing 'toward heaven still', but these days apple-picking is done (alas) without ladders, on dwarf trees in dwarf orchards. Still, it's a pleasure to eat a crisp, fresh apple straight from the tree, and nothing is better than the human hand when harvesting such delicate fruit.

Your reasons for picking apples will probably dictate where and what you pick. If you're picking apples for cider, for example, you might find yourself shovelling windfalls into sacks, along with any attendant wasps and cowpats. If you want apples for an apple pie, you might find yourself leaning over into a neighbour's garden to pluck a green cooker. If you want eating apples, you may end up on a pick-your-own farm: these begin trading from September onwards, and many farmers will plant a wide variety of trees for tasting purposes.

An apple every eight hours will keep three doctors away.

59.

MAKE ROSEHIP SYRUP

Rosehips are the fruit of the rose plant, and look like little fat bottles covered in lipstick. Come autumn, they can be used to make jellies, jams, syrup, soup or wine, and all species of rosehip are edible. They are not very palatable eaten raw, though: the inside of the hip contains a multitude of tiny hairs that can actually be used for itching powder, and they are known among country folk as 'itchy back berries'.

The easiest way to exploit hips is probably to make rosehip syrup. Just gather a good number of hips (leave a few on the plant, as they provide an important source of food for birds during the winter months), put them in a saucepan, and boil them with about twice their weight in water. They will soon begin to split and soften, at which point you can mash them with a potato masher. Simmer for half an hour, then strain through a cloth. Measure the resulting liquid, and add about three-quarters of the weight in sugar. Bring to the boil again, reduce to a thick syrupy consistency, then bottle in sterilised jars. Rosehip syrup is delicious on puddings, cereals or ice cream.

What is the connection between German submarines and rosehips? I'm glad you asked. Well, during World War II, Britain was starved of citrus fruits due to the blockade of goods arriving by sea. Nutritionists struck back, advising the populace that rosehips were a good alternative source of Vitamin C. Anyone who was a child in the war years will have memories of being fed homemade rosehip syrup.

60.

THROW A HALLOWEEN PARTY

Nowadays Halloween is thought to be an American import, but the USA is a pretty late arrival on the Halloween scene. All of the standard elements – trick-or-treating, apple-bobbing, bonfires, dressing up and so on – have their origins in European traditions (except perhaps the pumpkin – pre-1500 we used turnips). The name 'Halloween' comes from All Hallows' Eve, the night before All Hallows' Day on November 1st.

A Halloween party gives ample scope for fiendish creativity. First of all, decorations. Make sure the lighting is appropriate: use red, black or green lightbulbs to cast an unearthly glow. Consider having a flickering horror film playing in the background. Be liberal with effects such as fog (fog machines are not as expensive as you might think) and glow-in-the-dark spraypaint. Make fake gravestones with cardboard and write funny inscriptions on them. Or try a Psycho bathroom: buy a cheap shower curtain and slash it with a knife, leaving a fake knife on the sink, then spatter fake blood liberally around. Make sure you specify on your invitations whether or not your Halloween party is likely to be suitable for children!

Costumes are essential. Consider setting a theme for the party: axc murderers, tomb raiders, zombies, vampires, nuns (men love to dress as nuns), aliens. And play some Halloween games, traditional or new (try Guess the Body Part, in which guests must put their hands into covered boxes containing peeled lychees or jelly).

61.

CREATE YOUR OWN ALIEN COCOONS

You don't *have* to do this at Halloween, but it might look a little odd in April.

You'll need some balloons (black or white is best), some spraypaint and a roll of spiderwebbing. Rolls of artificial spider webbing can be bought from party supply shops.

First of all, choose a good spot: an entryway to a house, or perhaps a porch or pathway where trick-or-treaters will see your cocoons. Make sure there's a source of illumination, preferably a ghostly one. Inflate your alien sacs and wrap them individually with the spiderwebbing, making sure it clings tightly. Try making a few eggs that are different sizes: some aliens are the runts of the litter. Now paint the eggs. You can spraypaint them black or green, or use a brush to create streaks that look like veins or scales. Lay more spider webbing on top.

Arrange the eggs in bold clusters as if freshly laid by an insectoid alien. Tape them to the wall or fix them on nails; they can be high up or low on the ground. If they're outside, check they're not too much in the way of feet; and if there's a high wind, consider moving the display indoors. Drape some more spider webbing over them to stabilise the display.

Some alien goo might finish off the effect. This will give the impression of alien exudations, or perhaps the slime trail of a hatching alien. Goo can be bought from goo suppliers: alternatively use wallpaper paste and colouring.

62.

CARVE A PUMPKIN

The tradition of carving pumpkins, or Jack o' lanterns, originates from Ireland, where the vegetable involved was not a pumpkin but a turnip. The turnip was hollowed out and lit from within to ward off evil spirits and provide a handy light for wayfarers: the practice is almost certainly pre-Christian (associated with the festival of Samhain), but later there may have been an association with Catholic beliefs, the flickering lights representing the souls of the departed in purgatory.

Assembling the right tools will help greatly. First of all choose a very thin, serrated knife, possibly one designed for pumpkin carving. (A large, straight-edged knife is difficult to handle, and may slip, leading to more Halloween gore than you have planned.) For fine details, a sharp craft knife is good, though you won't want to give one to a child. A marker pen is also useful to sketch out your design on the skin.

You can design first on paper, then use the design as a template, poking through it with a knife to see where you need to cut. If you want something different from the traditional fanged face, you might like to try a more pictorial design such as a haunted house or a witch riding a broomstick. One tip: you don't always need to cut all the way through the pith. Just removing the orange skin to reveal the yellow flesh below creates a two-tone effect, and if the pith is thin enough, light will glow through it.

Use a tea-light for illumination, or, if you're particularly proud of your filigree-carving, illuminate the pumpkin from the front with a torch.

63.

ROAST PUMPKIN SEEDS

Once you've finished carving your pumpkin, you may feel in need of a snack. Luckily there's one on hand. Pumpkin seeds are delicious and nutritious (being full of zinc, antioxidants and vitamin E).

First of all, separate the seeds. This can be a time-consuming business, because the seeds are rather wedded to their slimy orange pulp. There's an easy way to do it, though: pull out the seeds *before* you remove the pulp from inside the pumpkin. With a gentle stroking action they will come out cleanly.

Now seasonings. Toss the seeds in oil: perhaps olive oil, or chilli oil, or sunflower oil, or whatever takes your fancy. Then, if you are not on a low-sodium diet, sprinkle a little salt. You can also add garlic powder, paprika, soy sauce, MSG or black pepper: you can even slather them in honey or maple syrup. Now roast in the oven on a medium heat until golden brown. You may need to turn them occasionally to ensure they are thoroughly done.

Pumpkin seeds are tasty eaten whole: you don't need to fuss with removing the casing if they are roasted thoroughly enough. Pumpkin seeds also make a nice addition to salads.

If you want to grow pumpkins for next year, set some seeds aside and dry them in a sunny place (or as sunny as you can find in November), then store in an airtight container until spring.

64.

BAKE A PUMPKIN PIE

Pumpkins are not really that edible. That's why you don't see them in the shops at any time other than Halloween, and why you're rarely served pumpkin in a restaurant (as opposed to, say, butternut squash, or any of pumpkin's tastier cousins). But in a highly processed form, pumpkin does very well.

To make the classic American pumpkin pie, you need, preferably, a culinary pumpkin specially bred for eating (not a half-rotten fibrous old monster with eyeholes hacked into it), 2 eggs, 25g/1oz melted butter, 165ml/6fl oz evaporated milk, 140g/5oz caster sugar, and some spices to taste, plus the ingredients for making shortcrust pastry (a ratio of 2 to 1 flour to fat, with a little water).

To prepare the flesh, skin and de-seed about 800g/2lb of the pumpkin, and simmer in water for half an hour until soft. Now push through a sieve to smooth out the texture, and blend it with the other ingredients. You can use maple syrup instead of sugar for a more American taste. Add spices such as cinnamon and nutmeg in half-teaspoon quantities. A teaspoon of vanilla adds creaminess.

Now make your pastry. Roll it out, put in in a 20cm/8in tart tin and blind bake it for 15 minutes at 180°C/Gas Mark 4, so that the crust is crisp. Put the pumpkin mixture into the tin and bake for a further 40 minutes at the same temperature. After this time the centre of the pie should have a feel like a set custard.

Serve with cream or ice cream. Quite a transformation.

65.

WAIT FOR THE GREAT PUMPKIN

In the *Peanuts* cartoons by Charles M Schulz, the character Linus van Pelt waits in a pumpkin patch every Halloween for the Great Pumpkin to appear. But the Great Pumpkin does not appear.

At one point in the animated film *It's the Great Pumpkin, Charlie Brown*, Linus is seen writing a letter to his gourd-deity: 'You must get discouraged because more people believe in Santa Claus than in you,' he scribbles. He pauses, and then adds: 'Well, let's face it, Santa Claus gets more publicity.' Linus is forced into the almost intolerable position of being in a religion of one. Yet he remains loyal year after year, never giving up hope, despite being derided by his crabby sister. His fidelity seems to be symbolic of humanity's yearning, against the odds, for a kindly, overwatching

Presence, even when that Presence is distinguished, most of the time, by Absence. Schulz himself wrote: 'I think life is full of anxieties and fears and tears. It has a lot of grief in it, and can be very grim. And I do not want to be the one who tries to tell somebody else what life is all about. To me it's a complete mystery.'

This autumn, then, join some of the *Peanuts* fans who eschew Halloween celebrations, forgo trick-or-treating, and stay away from Halloween parties and fancy dress. These people simply sit soberly in a pumpkin patch and wait in faith for a being who one day will come, confounding the doubters, a Halloween Messiah.

66.

HOLD A SÉANCE

Autumn, and particularly the transition from October to November, is a time in many cultures when the door to the Otherworld stands momentarily ajar. In the Celtic festival of Samhain, for instance, the dead are believed to visit the living, and food is set out for them. Fairies, spirits and imps can be heard gibbering and squeaking in the streets, and these are not just Halloween hen parties.

Autumn is an opportunity to communicate with the departed, therefore, by holding a séance.

To make sure your séance is a success, first of all vet your invitees, making sure they are willing to take it seriously. Nothing puts spirits off like a skeptic. Also make sure you've got a good number of people: six is excellent, since it's a multiple of three, a sacred number. Find a medium to lead the séance, someone who is experienced with unearthly entities. Set the scene carefully beforehand: dim the lighting, use a round table if possible, place some food in the centre of the table and a number of candles divisible by three. Turn off all phones. Then summon Them. Use a formula such as: 'Spirits of the dead, we attend you. Leave your world and come among us.' Wait for a sign that the invitation has been heard: a noise, a mutter, a rattle. Perhaps one of the guests may feel compelled to pass on a message. Ask questions of the spirit with yes or no answers: one rap for yes, two for no. When the séance is over, thank the spirits and ask them to pass back in peace to their domain.

Don't try to summon up evil beings. You may think you can handle it, but they are more evil than you are.

67.

HOLD A DUMB SUPPER

This is not a supper where you act like idiots. It's one where you don't speak. The idea, again, is to attract the spirits of the deceased, at a time of the year when ghosts and demons are believed (in some quarters) to be abroad. Dumb Suppers are an echo of centuries-old practices – which may, indeed, go back to the Stone Age, and are certainly found in Roman, Egyptian and Eastern religions – of offering food to spirits in the hope that they will either be propitiated or will communicate with the living.

Various Dumb Supper traditions exist. One is the Backwards Dumb Supper, where everything to do with the meal is performed backwards. The place settings are laid out with the knives and forks on the wrong side; the tablecloth is upside-down; the courses are served in reverse order, beginning with brandy and cigars and ending with an hors d'oeuvre. An extra place is laid for the departed person or the spirit who you desire to contact. At some point in the meal, the spirit will make its presence felt, perhaps by a gust of wind that blows the candles out, or a cat bounding onto the table. (If everyone has been silent for the last half an hour this can have quite an impact.) Alternatively there is the Black and White Dumb Supper, in which the table settings are exclusively black or white: black candles, white plates, black tablecloth, white napkins, and so on. Black and white food is consumed: liquorice, vanilla ice cream, black pudding and rice, etc. Perhaps not the most digestible of menus, but that's not the point.

68.

VISIT A VINEYARD

The grape harvest is in autumn, so there is no better time to visit a vineyard.

You might think there are no vineyards near you, but you'd be wrong. Vineyard planting in northern latitudes has come on apace in the last 30 years. In the UK, for example, there are now six times as many hectares planted with vines than in the 1970s. (Back then, all we had was 'British wine', which was a concoction made from imported grape juice concentrate. I can still remember the combination of sweetness and astringency, like blackcurrants marinated in diesel.)

Some vineyards allow visits, and some don't, so it's worth checking. If you're lucky you might find one where you can participate in the harvest yourself, and after the grape picking you might get a free lunch and a complimentary bottle of wine. Other vineyards offer river cruises or horse-drawn cart rides.

If you're just tasting, a little preparation will make your visit more enjoyable. Read up on the grapes planted and think of some questions to ask. Enquire, for example, about the harvest and how the grapes are judged ripe for picking; ask what factors make a good wine; or ask what makes a 'great' year as opposed to a merely 'good' one.

There's no obligation to buy, of course, but if you do purchase a bottle of something, you'll feel a special connection to it and will enjoy drinking it that much more.

If you're driving, remember to spit and not to swallow.

69.

MAKE HOT MULLED PERRY

This Halloween, while the children are scampering about the neighbourhood dressed as fairy streetwalkers or blood-spattered zombies – or after you have returned from doing the same – you'll need a nice warming drink. And nothing could be more authentically autumnal than hot mulled perry.

Perry is an ancient alcoholic drink originally made in the three English counties of Gloucestershire, Herefordshire and Worcestershire, but is now appreciated far and wide. It is, in its essence, cider made from pears. Real perry is made only from certain varieties of pear with a high tannin content, and the perry pear in its natural state is inedible (it's hard and astringent). Perry pears are pressed for their juice, which is fermented using the wild yeasts found on their skins. The different varieties of perry (formerly in their hundreds, though now sadly diminished due to the grubbing up of pear trees) have entertaining names: among them are Lumberskull, Merrylegs and Stinking Bishop (named after a malodorous perry-maker). The longest name recorded name for a perry is A Drop of That Which Hangs Over the Wall.

To make your mulled perry you need nothing more than a good farmhouse perry (not a mass-produced bottled variety which will often be made from pear concentrate or from dessert pears), plus some spices. Choose your own spices to taste: cinnamon, cloves, mace and nutmeg are popular. Just a little of each is sufficient. Put the spices in a muslin bag and leave to infuse in a saucepan of perry as you heat the liquid up. Do not bring the perry to the boil or you will lose alcohol content.

The most popular perry ever marketed was called Babycham, though no one who has sampled real perry wishes to remember the fact.

70.

GATHER SWEET CHESTNUTS

The Italians, Portuguese, French, Turks, South Koreans, Chinese and Japanese are all crazy about sweet chestnuts. In fact, the only countries that aren't are the British and Americans. Why, is a mystery. They're delicious, and if you gather them yourself, they're free.

What you are looking for is not the horse chestnut, or conker, which is inedible (except, presumably, by horses), but the edible chestnut. Mature chestnut trees are among the tallest woodland trees, with long spear-like leaves (completely different to the horse chestnut) and bark of a dull silvery brown. The nut itself looks superficially like the horse chestnut, but the green casings are not so much spiny as furry, and the nuts inside (two or three at a time) have a distinctive shape, flat on one side and hemispherical on the other, with a small pointed tip. They are ready for gathering from about October onwards.

Chestnuts in the nude are not pleasant to eat, but cooked they attain an entirely new dimension. The best way is probably to roast them. To do this, first of all pierce the shells to stop them exploding in the oven, and then, after about an hour's roasting, remove the shells: the inside is creamy, nutty and floury. Chestnuts can be eaten as sweets (such as marron glacés), chestnut soup, chestnut stuffing or as an ingredient in stews and sauces. Chestnuts can also be made into a flour which is particularly good for people with a gluten intolerance. A chestnut-flour cake is a real treat, perhaps served with some chestnut-milk custard.

71.

MAKE CRAB APPLE JELLY

The crab apple, or just the crab (a source of confusion in Shakespeare) is the small wild apple, commonly found growing in gardens as an ornamental tree. The fruit can be various colours, red, green or yellow, but surprisingly the jelly itself is always pink.

If you want to try your hand at making it, pick a few kilos of fruit, wash them and put them in a large saucepan. There's no need to core them or even to remove the stalks. Add enough water to cover them, and then boil until the apples have turned completely to pulp (half an hour should do). Now extract the juice from the pulp. This requires patience and some muslin. Spread the muslin (or other fairly loosely woven cloth) in a colander and add the pulp. Don't press it, or you will get a cloudy juice – just leave it overnight. The juice will drain out of the pulp and you will be left with a clear liquid.

When the juice has expressed itself, measure it and add three-quarters by weight of sugar. This high sugar content offsets the very high acidity of the juice. Bring this liquid back to the boil and reduce it to the point where the jelly will set on the back of a cold spoon, or in a cold saucer. You're now ready to bottle up. Any containers will do, as long as they're clean.

Crab apple jelly is a versatile condiment – it can be spread on toast, used to flavour puddings, or served with roast meat. It's a perfect accompaniment to autumn feasts and festivals.

72.

FALL IN LOVE

> Autumn, that wild season when rural men rack
> orchard trees with sticks and weep with the desire to
> kiss faraway Demeter's supple breasts – to set lips to
> her travel-swollen eyes.
> – Roman Payne, *Rooftop Soliloquy*

What better time to fall in love than Fall? The year is gently dying. Each leaf is a death poem. People wrapped in scarves beg one another with silent eyes to heal the disappointments of summer.

Autumn is made for love. But it's a subtle sort of love. An autumn love is not celebratory and half-naked. It is not about roses, chocolates and teddy bears, and shops festooned in pink. An autumn romance encompasses fading photographs, distant music, letters written with cartridge pens, broken tombstones, woodsmoke, leaves pressed between pages of a book, and things unspoken (or perhaps unspeakable). Autumnal love is passion tinged with grief.

And of course it's in autumn that you're most likely to meet someone. When do university courses start? Autumn. When do you go back to school? Autumn. When do you decide to try a new career? When change is in the air, in autumn. New people, new opportunities to fall in love.

If you do not fall in love this autumn, you may fall in love with love itself.

73.

BOB FOR APPLES

Bobbing for apples is a centuries-old Halloween tradition. It may be connected with the Roman goddess Pomona, who brought the gift of fruit trees to the British Isles: or it may be of even greater antiquity (there is an intriguing suggestion that the pentagonal shape formed by the core when you slice an apple in half led pre-Christian people to regard the apple as a sacred fruit).

The basics of apple bobbing are simple: find a large tub, fill it with water, and place a few apples in it. Apples are lighter than water: if you get one that sinks, discard it as a biohazard. Players, hands behind their backs, try and catch an apple with their teeth, or compete individually with thirty seconds apiece.

Apple bobbing is associated with divination. The folklore historian William Henry Davenport Adams described the game as follows in his *Curiosities of Superstition* (1882):

> [The apples] are thrown into a tub of water, and you endeavour to catch one in your mouth as they bob round and round in provoking fashion. When you have caught one, you peel it carefully, and pass the long strip of peel thrice, sunwise, round your head; after which you throw it over your shoulder, and it falls to the ground in the shape of the initial letter of your true love's name.

Other divination games associated with Halloween include placing a row of nuts by the fire, and naming each one after a prospective lover. If a nut burns with a steady glow, it symbolises the constant flame of true love. If it explodes, it symbolises the ecstatic detonation of a sudden passion. Halloween in some parts has accordingly been called 'Nutcrack Night'.

74.

GO PUNKIN CHUNKIN

Where: Bridgeville, Delaware, USA; Bikschote, Belgium; elsewhere
When: November
Who: People who thrill when things go far and then splatter
Equipment: Arm, sling, trebuchet or compressed air gun; pumpkin
How often: Annual; since 1986

The World Championship 'Punkin Chunkin' ('punkin' here is 'pumpkin', and 'chunkin' is … well, a new verb made up for the occasion) is in Delaware, USA, but you can do it anywhere, and since 2004 there have been European championships in Belgium.

It began in 1986 when a couple of guys started throwing pumpkins around in a field. Soon they progressed to using catapults and other machines. Now 30,000 people turn out annually to watch and take part in what has become a phenomenon of autumnal absurdity. The 'World Championship Punkin Chunkin' regularly grosses more than $100,000 in ticket sales and other revenue, much of which is donated to charity. Competitors are divided into categories including Human Powered, Trebuchet, Catapult, Centrifugal and Air Cannon (with other divisions for Female Air Cannon, Youth Human Powered etc), and the machines are capable of throwing melons, pumpkins, deep-fried turkeys and cats. In one championship event a team was disqualified for using compressed helium.

The most successful pumpkin gun so far is 'The Big 10 Inch' pneumatic cannon, a behemoth whose best shot is well over a mile (more exactly 5,545 feet, or 1,690m). Other recent winners include the Second Amendment, the Hormone Blaster, and the Q36 Pumpkin Modulator.

75.

TAKE A BET ON THE MAN BOOKER

The Man Booker Prize for Fiction is a prize of £50,000 awarded every October for the best novel in English published that year. Winners have included Salman Rushdie, Kazuo Ishiguro and Hilary Mantel (twice, at the time of writing). It's the biggest event of the literary calendar, looming so large, in fact, that some have seen its influence as pernicious: the journalist Richard Gott pronounced it 'a significant and dangerous iceberg in the sea of British culture that serves as a symbol of its current malaise'.

The Man Booker is open to citizens of the Commonwealth, Ireland and Zimbabwe, but not the rest of the world. However, there is also a Man Booker International Prize, worth even more money – £60,000 – and awarded biennially, also in October, which is open to anyone writing in, or whose writing has been translated into, English. The international prize is slightly different in that it doesn't reward a particular novel, but a novelist's overall contribution to literary culture. Winners have included Philip Roth, Chinua Achebe and Alice Munro.

So, if you want to take a punt, there are two prizes to choose from this October. As soon as the shortlist is announced, get down to the shops, buy all the books, devour them, judge them and take your pick. Bookmakers will have the odds all ready.

Hopefully you will win enough to cover the cost of buying the books.

76.

BUY YOUR CHRISTMAS PRESENTS EARLY

If some theologians are to be believed, we should all be celebrating Christmas in autumn rather than winter. The nativity was probably not on the 25th of December, but some time in October.

This aside, preparing early for Christmas has many advantages. The most obvious comes when shopping online. Around the 1st of December, online shoppers begin to assail retailers with orders, and frankly, retailers struggle to keep up. Most of us have had the experience of ordering a gift in December and receiving it in February. Then there is the creaking postal service. The mails put on extra staff, but they are underpaid and overworked, and not a few deliveries end up in snowdrifts or cached under railway embankments.

If you shop for Christmas in autumn, you can relax and enjoy it. Acquire a gift here, a gift there, and spread the cost and the labour. Browse in September, buy in October, wrap in November. (Don't leave your presents too long without gift tags, though, or you will have to unwrap them to see whose is whose.)

It would be nice to be able to apply the principle to the entirety of Christmas, but a tree bought in October may not have many needles left by Christmas Day.

77.

SEE A SKEIN OF GEESE

Geese are migratory birds, and one of the most stirring sights of autumn is to see them flying over salt marshes or estuaries in characteristic skeins (V-formations), honking as they go.

Geese tend to breed in the Arctic Circle, Scandinavia, Greenland and Canada. They then migrate to warmer climes, arriving in central Europe to fatten up around September. Barnacle geese, pink-footed geese, white-fronted geese, Canada geese, greylag geese, bean geese and Brent geese, all visit in huge numbers. At Martin Mere in the north-west of England, 20,000 to 30,000 pink-footed geese regularly touch down in the autumn. You can watch it happen. In Scotland, the best places are along the Solway Coast, the Loch of Strathbeg and the Loch of Leven; in Wales along the Severn Estuary; and in Ireland on the west coast near counties Mayo and Sligo.

Why do geese and other birds fly in skeins? It's a question of aerodynamics. Each bird in the V (except the leader) flies in the lift created by the small turbulences that form at the wingtips of the bird ahead. This gives a significant reduction in drag, allowing the birds to fly longer distances.

As well as flying in skeins, you will also see geese whiffling. This extraordinary behaviour is when geese drop like dead weights from the sky in order to land quickly. They may even be upside-down as they fall, then regain control just before landing. Like a judge riding a bicycle, a whiffling goose manages to be both ungainly and graceful at the same time.

78.

CALL A DUCK

Continuing with the wildfowl theme, the idea of duck calling is to produce duck-like sounds to attract migrating ducks and kill them with guns. The Duck Calling World Championships are held every autumn in Stuttgart, Arkansas, USA, and as the name suggests, participants from all around the world are invited (rather like the World Series in baseball, where there are admittedly not many foreign entrants, but they are welcomed in principle). In the first Championships of 1924, the winner, Mr D Walsh, took home a hunting coat valued at $6.60. Now the affair is a fiesta of extraordinary proportions, generating huge revenues and doling out thousand-dollar prizes. As with many similar festivals there is a proliferation of supporting events: these include the Duck Dog contest, the Duck Gumbo Cook-Off, the Duck Widows Tennis Tournament and Queen

Mallard and Junior Queen Mallard, a beauty contest (for human females).

If you want to have a go at duck calling yourself, you will need a duck call, the device that makes duck noises. This is a short instrument like a kazoo containing a reed. By making noises into the instrument like 'konc, konc, konc' or 'tikkitikkitikki' you can imitate the various species of ducks – teal, mallard, pintail, wigeon, etc – in their various moods. Duck calling calls include the Basic Quack, the Greeting Call, the Hail Call, the Comeback, the Feed Call and the Lonesome Hen.

Manufacturers of duck calls include the company Redneck Pride, whose slogan is 'Sounds so real they will think you are one'.

79.

KICK LEAVES

Autumn, in some countries, is Fall. Fall of leaves. The season is defined by its lost leaves.

In his poem *Spring and Fall* Gerard Manley Hopkins asked:

> Margaret, are you grieving
> Over Goldengrove unleaving?

As Hopkins and Margaret knew, autumn does bring with it feelings of heartache. The leaves are the leaves of loss, the loss of another year's freshness. Margaret was rooted to the spot with doleful imaginings, 'unleaving' as the trees unleaved themselves.

But autumn may also be a season for joy, even as one watches the leaves tumble. To see how leaves dance in the wind, flocks of them borne up to spiral and careen around you, a kaleidoscope of reds, browns, yellows, and oranges, is one of the delights of the year.

So in this spirit, kick the leaves this autumn. Raise them in detonations of gold: cover your friends with leaves. Ride a bike through them, and, letting one foot slip from the pedal, drive a flying trough through them as you go. Celebrate as the trees undress.

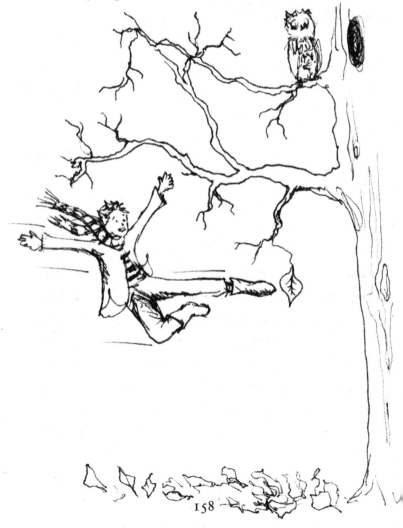

80.

GATHER BEECHNUTS

Beechnuts are, as the name suggests, the nuts of the beech tree, and are plentiful in autumn. They are the lobster of the wild wood. That is, they take much effort to harvest and unshell, but a tasty treat lies within (and it is in the very labour of uncovering the meat that half the enjoyment lies).

Beechnuts are unmistakable, so there is no risk of poisoning. You don't even need to be able to identify a beech tree. Just look for the fallen casings. These are small, about the size of a penny piece, a drab brown, and spiny. By the time they reach the ground they have usually cracked and split open, revealing the twin nuts within, or perhaps have shed their nuts out onto the ground in the act of falling. These nuts are your quarry. They are very small – less than half an inch (1cm) long – and have three sides, one wider than the other two. If you imagine a beechnut lying on its widest side, it would look like a tiny one-man tent, the colour of ancient shoe leather.

To reach the kernel, use your thumbnail to score a line down the widest of the three sides, and peel off the outer skin. Exposed is the fleshy yellow nut. Pop it in. It has an oily, woody taste. Immediately you want another one, then another ... and before long you are tethered beneath the boughs of the beech tree, savouring the taste of autumn as the day scuds by ...

81.

GO MOON-VIEWING

In many cultures, the full moons of autumn are considered especially large and bright: our own culture celebrates the harvest moon. Autumn is an ideal pretext for moon-viewing.

You don't need a telescope to observe the moon. Normal eyesight will do quite well. Wait until the full moon, and if you are lucky enough to have clear skies, take a hike to a dark place where the moon can be seen in all its glory. Light pollution is not such a problem with moon-viewing as with star-gazing, but it's still best to find as dark a spot as possible.

You'll be able to see the lunar seas, the dark patches which are not 'seas', as such, or the relics of seas, but wide plains formed by volcanic eruptions. Because the moon always keeps the same side turned to the earth, it's possible to name them with some confidence: on the right side, descending, are the sea of serenity, the sea of tranquility and the sea of fecundity, and on the left side are the sea of showers and the ocean of storms. Those with exceptional eyesight (and perhaps a pair of binoculars) will be able to see craters too, particularly Kepler crater, top centre, and Tycho crater, bottom centre.

In 2000, a study published in the British Medical Journal counted the number of dog-bite admissions to two hospitals during the full moon, one hospital in Birmingham and one in Australia. The Birmingham hospital showed double the usual number of admissions, while the Australian hospital showed half. A rather lunatic result.

82.

PLAY CONKERS

Nigel Molesworth in *How to be Topp* is a big conkers enthusiast, though he blenches at declaring, on finding the first conker of the season:

> Oddly oddly onker, my first conker.

It's extraordinary how conkers resonate in the memory. Freshly fallen from the tree, slick with the fine oil from their pith, they are objects of great beauty. Boys, particularly, seem driven to collect hundreds of them, hoarding them in boxes that they hide under their beds. And then the lip-biting concentration of drilling through the meat of the conker with a nail, hoping not to crack it; the ritual of baking or soaking in vinegar to harden the nut (both illegal in many jurisdictions); and the game itself with its many improvised 'rules' (you can cry 'stamps!' and jump on your opponent's conker if you knock it to the ground, but if your opponent cries 'no stamps!' you must refrain). Conkers may not be sweet chestnuts but victory is sweet.

At the world conker championships at Ashton, Northamptonshire, on the second Sunday of October, contestants vie for the title of 'Conkerer' but are not allowed to bring their own nuts; instead, to prevent cheating, they are allotted a conker by the organisers. This, surely, removes the whole point, which is the thrill of owning a legendary victor, the equivalent of an ancient battle mace, that has accumulated many 'lives' (becoming a six-er, seven-er, eight-er or more).

Sorry, Ashton!

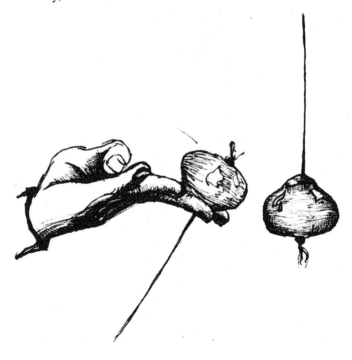

83.

GO TO A HARVEST FESTIVAL

The word 'harvest' comes from old English 'haerfest', which means 'autumn'; so, in a sense, harvest and autumn are identical.

Harvest festivals are held in many places around the world, and occur at different times of the year. The Indian harvest festival of Pongal, for example is held in January. In Western Europe and the US, harvest occurs in September or October. In Britain, schools and churches are decorated with sheaves of grain, agricultural products and, often, tinned food (which has led to much childish confusion as to whether baked beans can be harvested by the cylinder). Harvest festivals are now often centred on charitable activity to support developing counties, and are less the riot of alcohol and coupling than they were in the agrarian past.

One place in Britain where a traditional harvest festival survives is in Cornwall, where 'crying the neck' is celebrated at harvest. The 'neck' is the last sheaf of wheat left standing at the end of the harvest. The cutting of the neck and its 'crying' (or public cheering) is followed by Guldize, which involves a procession, music and feasting. One tradition of Guldize is that a farmhand carrying the neck must run as fast as he can to the farmhouse, and try to enter without being spotted by a female guard (a dairymaid or other wench). The guard is armed with a bucket of water, and if she catches him, she soaks him: if he gets in without being wetted, he is entitled to receive a kiss.

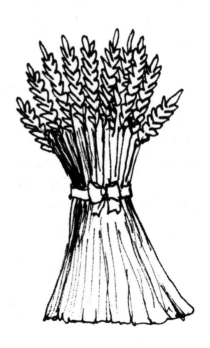

84.

GO TO AN ALTERNATIVE HARVEST FESTIVAL

In China, Taiwan and Vietnam, and in expatriate communities around the world (the USA, Canada, Australia and elsewhere), the mid-autumn festival, held in September or October, is among the liveliest celebrations of the year.

In Vietnam, the mid-autumn festival is especially associated with children. Children, in their innocence and joy, are held to be closer to the gods, and the festival celebrates them with lantern parades and masks. There are many legends and stories connected with the festival. One concerns a villager, Cuoi, whose wife urinated on a magical tree. The tree, in indignation, rose to heaven, and Cuoi tried to pull it back to earth. Unfortunately, he was carried to heaven with it and couldn't get back. The lantern parades of the children are a perennial attempt to lead poor Cuoi back home.

Those of a more austere bent celebrate the festival with poetry, song, and contemplation of the moon. Among the Zhuang people of China, the full moon is the central feature of the mid-autumn festival: the sun and moon are conceived to be lovers, and when the moon waxes at harvest time she is pregnant with stars. Elsewhere there is a focus on mooncakes, sweet round cakes that symbolise plenty and family unity. In some traditions, thirteen mooncakes of diminishing sizes, representing the thirteen months of the lunar year, are piled on top of one another like a pagoda.

85.

MAKE CIDER

To make cider you need cider apples. These are rather surprising little beasts. They are small and hard, and they taste (for the most part) pretty poisonous. Yet, when juiced, they yield a sweet, thick, syrupy liquid. Most cidermakers prefer to mix a few varieties of apples in their brew, which is the reason why farm cider tastes different everywhere you go.

After you've got your hands on some cider apples, you need to pulp them. This can be accomplished by hand, but you will more likely need a mechanical or electric pulper (don't do it in a blender; you will set fire to the house).

Now strain the pulp to get the juice. You need to put a lot of pressure on apple pulp to get the first, let alone the last oozings, so again, a press of some kind is called for. The equipment price tag is going up, but it'll be worth it.

When you've got your juice, you need to start the first fermentation in a single large container such as a fermentation bin or barrel. Add a yeast culture: champagne yeast is often used for cider, possibly because cider is the champagne of the downtrodden. (By the way, you can make sparkling cider too, which is every bit as good as champagne).

After a few days, fermentation will have ceased and the cider can be transferred to bottles or polypins. It must then be left for a good few weeks for the best results. This is a severe test of character. If autumn can teach you anything, it is that good things come to those who wait.

86.

MAKE SLOE GIN

Sloe gin is a bit of a cheat. It involves three ingredients, two of them bought from a shop, and one of which will get you drunk already. They are sloes, sugar and gin. Why not just drink the gin, you may ask, perhaps with some tonic and a slice of lemon? Well, the answer is that sloe gin can be a wonderfully warming drink, a sort of hyper-charged port.

Sloes are the fruit of the blackthorn tree, which grows prolifically in the British countryside and elsewhere around the world. It has slender dark branches and white flowers in spring, and gets its name from its vicious spikes. The fruits, which are usually harvested from October onwards, are round, about a centimetre in diameter, and a deep imperial purple. Like cider apples or elderberries, or anything else that you make alcohol out of, they are inedible in the raw state, and if you try to eat them their astringency is such that you will feel as if someone has superglued your tongue to your teeth.

The method of making it is simple: pick as many sloes as you like and add half their weight in sugar, and then double their weight in gin. So, for example, if you have (in metric) 500g of sloes, add 250g of sugar and 1 litre of gin. Put them in a resealable jar and turn the jar every day to mix them up. After about three months, strain out the sloes and sediment, bottle the concoction, and store in a dark place.

Sloe gin: sloe by name, slow by nature. The longer you leave it, the better it will be.

87.

MAKE BLACKBERRY WINE

Cider, gin and wine completes your alcoholic autumn triad. Blackberries are the most abundant of the free autumn fruits, and they make a delicious home brew.

Pick blackberries, of all shapes and descriptions. They are going into a drink rather than a pie, so a few red or rotten ones won't hurt. Weigh them when you've finished, and put them into a large fermenting bin or bucket (available at homebrew shops). Add two-thirds of their weight in sugar and double their weight in boiling water. For example, if you've got (in metric) three kilograms of blackberries, add two kilograms of sugar and six litres of water. Stir the mixture thoroughly, mashing the blackberries as you go, then leave to cool. Add a teaspoon of pectolytic enzyme so that the mixture will clear at a later stage, plus some wine yeast. You can use a hydrometer at this point (another piece of kit available at homebrew shops) to check the starting sugar content of the brew, but the hydrometer really comes into its own as fermentation occurs. When the hydrometer has dipped down to zero after a few days, you will know that fermentation has finished. One tip: try using a fermentation belt around the bucket to bring the brew to a good temperature.

Strain into demijohns and leave to bubble for a month. After that, transfer to bottles. If you make your blackberry wine in September it will be ready for a toast around the Christmas goose.

88.

TREAT YOURSELF TO A PUMPKIN FACIAL

After the ravages to your skin caused by seasonal excess, you may wish to prepare a pumpkin face mask to soothe, exfoliate and replenish.

Pumpkin is actually a serious contender when it comes to skin treatments. It contains various useful substances such as vitamins A, C and E, beta carotene, zinc, potassium and antioxidants. Applied with care, it should leave your skin feeling fresher, suppler and more moisturised.

To prepare the facial, first find some pumpkin flesh (there should be plenty of it hanging around). Cook it thoroughly by simmering in water, and then force it through a sieve, eliminating strings and seeds. (You can also cook in a microwave with a little water in the bowl.) Take around half a cup of this and mix it with an egg and a tablespoon of milk. (Variants on the recipe call for yoghurt, olive oil and honey.) Now invite friends round for a Halloween cosmetology party. Using a brush, take it in turns to apply the mixture to one another's faces, making sure it doesn't go in the eyes. Leave it on for about fifteen minutes (the facial will dry and crack as it is absorbed, but that's normal) and then wash off.

Instead of the traditional cucumber placed over each eye, you could put a maple leaf.

89.

CONTEMPLATE TRANSIENCE

Everything changes. You can't stand in the same river twice. At least you can, but you'll need two changes of socks.

There is much to be gained from contemplating transience. A heroine in a Chekhov short story had a ring on which was engraved the words: 'All must pass.' This made her melancholy in happy times but cheered her up in sad times. If you develop the habit of looking at life as transient, it's amazing how your problems come into perspective. Today you must pay your taxes, buy a new cooker, repair a dripping tap, and these problems may be causing you considerable stress. But in a year's time you will almost certainly have forgotten all about them. Were they really worth the stress? Get into the habit of asking yourself this: in a year's time, will this problem be important?

Autumn is the ideal time to contemplate transience.

Summer is over. It was brash and short-lived, and hardly very mindful. Now is the time to appreciate the beauty of things as they change, and appreciate that their beauty lies partly in their mutability. Try a simple meditation that involves sitting in a quiet place and contemplating. Your blood pressure will lower, your emotional stability will improve, your fears and phobias will decrease, and you will certainly be more tolerant of the people who normally infuriate you. You will learn to accept who they, and you, are.

This is worth a thousand summers.

90.

MAKE A BLACKBERRY AND APPLE PIE

Both blackberries and apples come into their own in autumn, so it's an irresistible combination.

First of all, as Mrs Beeton would say, catch your blackberry. There's no right way to do this. Many people will have memories of blackberrying from childhood: in my own case, they were growing on the concrete banks of a drainage canal that passed under several busy roads. But no one, it seemed, had thought of going down there to get them, and they were the biggest, sweetest, most luscious blackberries imaginable – and there were thousands of them. It's true: the best blackberries are always somehow the most inaccessible ones, either too high up to reach or too deep in the jungle to penetrate without being scratched raw.

Once you've got your blackberries, you need an apple or two. Cooking apples, naturally: scrumped apples, preferably. A blackberry and apple pie should be free, bar the pastry.

Bring your ingredients home, and with bleeding forearms prepare your pie. Shortcrust pastry is simple. Plain flour and butter in a ratio of 2:1, plus a pinch of salt. Line the pie dish with the pastry and add the apples, thickly sliced and raw, and the blackberries, washed. Sprinkle with sugar to taste. Cover the pie with pastry, glaze with egg if you're feeling fancy, and bake for 25-30 minutes on 200°C/400°F/Gas 6. Serve with custard or cream.

91.

GIVE THANKS

The first thanksgiving was celebrated by ... well, it all depends on who you believe. It could have been Puritan colonists in New England in the 1620s, or earlier Spanish colonists in the American West. It could even have been Columbus. These first celebrants were giving thanks to God for survival in a strange land. Nothing cheers you up like turkey with cranberry sauce and pumpkin pie.

The modern holiday, celebrated on the last Thursday in November, is not exclusively an American affair: it's also celebrated in Canada, and anywhere else in the world where Americans or Canadians congregate. If you know any Americans or Canadians, get them to invite you!

One animal that has little cause to celebrate is the turkey. Except that every year one lucky bird is presented to the president of the United States by the

National Turkey Federation and officially 'pardoned'. This tradition began with President Kennedy, who spared a live bird presented to him in 1963. It was made into an official pardon during the presidency of Ronald Reagan, who, when asked questions by journalists about pardoning Oliver North during the Iran-Contra affair in 1987, joked that he had just pardoned a turkey named Charlie. Nowadays turkeys are specially selected for 'pardoning' from a young age and are trained to deal with flashing lights and large crowds. A vice-turkey is also groomed for the job in case the main turkey falls ill before the ceremony, and after being pardoned, both turkeys are sent to Disneyland where they live out the rest of their natural lives.

If this sounds unbelievable, remember that truth is stranger than fiction.

92.

DEEP FRY A TURKEY

If you are not planning to pardon your turkey, you have several cooking options.

Deep frying a turkey has one main advantage: it's quick. A turkey can be cooked in 40 minutes rather than the three hours it would take in an oven. Deep frying a turkey also has one main disadvantage: it's dangerous. You could create a twenty-foot-high fireball that would destroy your house.

Of course not all Americans burn their houses down, so some of them must be doing it right. The chief thing to do is to get the right equipment. This comprises: a burner supplied with gas from a cylinder; a made-for-purpose pot; a CO_2 fire extinguisher; an oil thermometer; a meat thermometer; and some wire to act as a harness when lowering the turkey into the pot. Never deep-fry indoors: always do it outdoors away from buildings and children. Also, never deep fry a frozen turkey.

Estimate the amount of oil you will need by first submerging the turkey in cold oil. The oil should cover the turkey and yet be at least 6 inches from the rim of the pot. Remove the turkey from the cold oil and fire up the gas until the oil reaches 350°F (175°C). Turn the burner off: if there are any overspills, the oil can't now catch fire. Having inserted the wire harness through the turkey's ribcage and legs, making sure it is super-secure, lower the bird into the boiling oil. Allow a cooking time of 4 minutes per pound (500g) of turkey, but don't use a bird over 6kg (12lb): it won't cook without burning the skin. After 45 minutes, test the bird with a meat thermometer to make sure it is piping hot inside.

Happy deep-fried Thanksgiving!

93.

INDULGE IN A FRENZY OF CONSUMERISM ...

... on Black Friday. This is the day after Thanksgiving in the American calendar. Because Thanksgiving always falls on a Thursday (the last Thursday in November), Black Friday is, for many non-retail workers, an unofficial public holiday before the weekend, and an opportunity to do a bit of shopping. Or actually a lot of shopping, because Black Friday has been for many years the most commercially active of any date in the year. The term Black Friday has now spread throughout the world, even in places where no one celebrates Thanksgiving.

Why 'Black'? Unfortunately the name originally had negative connotations, as in 'black-hearted' or 'a black day'. Everyone had the day off and everyone wanted to shop, and so traffic built up to intolerable levels, bringing American cities to a standstill. In a triumph of re-branding, however, the term 'black' was later glossed as 'in profit' and the day acquired a more politically correct cast.

Violence has dogged Black Friday. In one case, an impatient gang of shoppers trampled a store employee to death; on another black day (in the original sense) a US marine collecting 'Toys for Tots' at a mall was stabbed; on yet another a woman waiting for an Xbox attacked her rival consumers with pepper spray.

Better perhaps, to stay at home and celebrate 'Cyber Monday', instead, the Monday following Black Friday when online sales reach their peak (see §76, 'Buy your Christmas presents early').

94.

OBSERVE BUY NOTHING DAY

The antithesis to Black Friday is Buy Nothing Day, and, conveniently, it falls on the same day. In countries with no Thanksgiving, Buy Nothing Day is sometimes shifted to the next day, i.e. Saturday.

Buy Nothing Day emerged in the early 1990s as a campaign by the Canadian magazine *Adbusters* ('the journal of the mental environment'). The day's philosophy is simple: on Buy Nothing Day, buy nothing. Cut up your credit card if necessary. Proponents of the day argue that rampant consumerism has an environmental impact, with 80% of the earth's resources being consumed by 20% of the population. This madness, they say, must cease.

In the early years of Buy Nothing Day, supporters tried to run TV 'uncommercials' promoting the day of inaction, but TV channels refused to run the ads, and a spokesman for CBS commented: 'This commercial is in opposition to the current economic policy of the United States.'

Nevertheless Buy Nothing Day took off and become bigger (or smaller) every year, with ever-increasing volumes of non-sales. Buy Nothing protesters also organised events such as the Trolley Slump, a version of the Trolley Dash in which hundreds of participants take over a store, each pushing one empty trolley slowly around and around, bringing ordinary retail activity to a standstill.

Buy Nothing Day is referred to by some supporters as 'Occupy Christmas'.

95.

GIVE UNTHANKS

If you don't feel like giving thanks, and American holidays give you the pip, you can celebrate Unthanksgiving Day. This falls every year on the same day as Thanksgiving (the last Thursday in November) and is a traditional day of protest by Native American groups, seeking to draw attention to the trauma of European colonisation, in which millions of indigenous people died from genocidal wars and disease.

The first Unthanksgiving Day was on November 20, 1969, during the height of the Civil Rights movement. A group of Native American activists, the Alcatraz Red Power Movement, inspired by a treaty of 1868 which stated that any land not used by the US government automatically reverted to the control of indigenous peoples, occupied Alcatraz Island in San Francisco Bay. (Alcatraz was no longer in use as a prison island and was thus effectively surplus land.) The occupation lasted for one-and-a-half years and was only ended when government agents stormed the island.

Since then, a ceremony has been held at dawn on the island, involving dancing, speeches and revelry. Control of the event has now passed to the International Indian Treaty Council and is now known more commonly as the Sunrise Gathering. The aim nowadays is to celebrate the survival of indigenous peoples from both North and South America against what seemed at times very short odds. It's open to the general public, and boat trips leave from Fisherman's Wharf early on Thanksgiving morn, when most Americans are still in bed dreaming of burning the house down (see §92).

96.

LEARN A NEW SKILL

Autumn is a time for learning something new. Everyone's doing it. In autumn, people go back to school or college, start new jobs, return from summer holidays with resolutions to change their lives (ditch the partner, start a bar in Alicante). It's the natural time to reassess a life.

You can divide your potential learning into three areas: work skills, home skills and self-improvement skills.

If you're interested in honing your work skills, look first of all at the magic boxes that rule our lives: computers. If you can add proficiency in spreadsheets or web design to your CV, it will probably benefit you more than anything else.

At home, there are plenty of options. DIY, textiles, photography, interior design, painting and decorating. Then, once you've got your home to a state approaching

Vogue readiness, think about renting parts of it out. There are various websites now (Air BnB, Wimdu, HomeAway) where you can invite strangers into your home, give them breakfast and accept banknotes.

For self-improvement, the top pick has to be languages. Learning a language opens more doors than any other skill: a new language can land you a new job, a new relationship, a new holiday destination, or a new life.

Or you could learn how to learn. This isn't as silly as it sounds. Thinking first about learning methods and your personal learning style could immensely improve the confidence and efficiency with which you learn something new, and there are courses to teach you how to do it.

97.

LIVE LONGER – EAT NUTS

Certain autumnal activities can extend your life. Eating seasonal nuts is one of them. There is now well-established research proving that nuts protect against coronary heart disease. In addition, nuts are recommended by doctors for patients with some types of diabetes, and can reduce low-density lipoprotein cholesterol concentrations (often called 'bad cholesterol'). Nuts also contain essential fatty acids and are rich in minerals such as selenium, magnesium, potassium and phosphorus. One recent study found that frequent consumption of nuts led to a two year increase in life expectancy, mainly due to a decrease in coronary and cholesterol problems, but also because of their importance in maintaining vitamin E levels (vitamin E being an important antioxidant).

If you wish to extend your life (though it probably won't work if you are simultaneously smoking, drinking and pursuing extreme sports) then raw nuts are better than roasted ones: the roasting process boils off some of the oil that is efficacious in the life-lengthening stakes.

You would be well advised to act like a squirrel and start hoarding now.

98.

AID FROGS AND TOADS

The best way to do this is to build a garden pond. Nowadays, as a result of new fashions in garden design, there are significantly fewer garden ponds than there used to be.

Building a pond in autumn is a good idea: by spring, when frogs and toads spawn, the pond will be a fully functioning ecosystem, and not just a hole in the ground filled with tap water.

The size of the pond will dictate whether you get frogs or toads. Frogs can make do with a puddle or a bucket full of rainwater, whereas toads need a larger body of water.

So, after considering how big you want to go, mark out the pond and dig a hole that is deep at one end, so that the bottom remains unfrozen in winter, and has shallow edges. The edges are to allow amphibians to get in and out easily, and also to stop other garden creatures such as hedgehogs falling in and drowning. Buy a rubberised pond liner of the required size and lay it in, previously having removed any sharp stones from the hole. Fill with a hose. Now 'seed' the pond by taking some water from a natural ancient pond in a wild place. Just fill up a couple of empty drinks bottles with the natural pond water and tip them in. (Don't do this with water from another garden pond, since it may have problems with disease.)

Add some plants such as water lilies or water irises. Don't add fish; they eat tadpoles. Now wait for frogs and toads to arrive. By spring, your garden will be filled with the serenades of amphibians in love.

99.

CELEBRATE DIWALI

Diwali, or Deepavali, is a five-day festival celebrated by Hindus, Sikhs and Jains, and takes place between mid-October and mid-November. Diwali is often translated as 'the festival of lights', and one of its central activities is the lighting of Diwali candles or *diya* which are set outside homes, arranged in beautiful patterns, or floated down rivers. Other activities include the exchanging of special sweets such as *barfi* and *ladoo*, the detonation of fireworks, the creation of patterns known as *rangoli* using coloured powder, and the wearing of flower garlands. The goddess Lakshmi, the bringer of wealth and good fortune, is particularly associated with the festival. Many Indian businesses start their financial year on the first day of Diwali.

In recent years Diwali has become a truly international festival, in which people of all faiths or none can happily take part. Diwali celebrations are now prominent in the United States, Australia, Canada, New Zealand and Britain, as well as in countries with large Hindu, Sikh or Jain populations (India, Sri Lanka, Thailand, and so on). In Britain, Diwali happily coincides with both Halloween and Bonfire Night, and the two festivals merge seamlessly in some parts of the East End of London.

Diwali may be, on one level, about the desire for wealth and prosperity, but it also has a theological dimension to do with light. At Diwali, goodness and truth are asserted over the forces of evil and lies; justice and mercy triumph over misdeeds and cruelty.

100.

PICK MUSHROOMS

The anthropologist Claude Levi-Strauss wrote that Europe was divided into mycophobes (mushroom-haters) and mycophiles (mushroom-lovers): Britain and the Germanic countries are among the mycophobes, and France, Italy and the Slavic countries among the mycophiles. It's certainly true that most British people can't name more than a couple of mushroom species, let alone confidently identify them, while many Italians or Czechs can name and identify dozens.

If you want to try gathering wild mushrooms (and autumn, of course, is when mushroom-hunting comes into its own), then first of all get a good field guide. There are dozens of tasty fungi, and not a few others that will give you a seriously bad day. Take the guide with you, familiarise yourself with mushroom anatomy, learn about mushroom habitats (some mushrooms prefer pasture, others woodland, some mushrooms prefer to root at the base of particular trees, etc) and learn some Latin terms.

Your best protection against picking something that will not sit well in an omelette, or in your nervous system, is to get to know a few safe species and then stick to them. A good starter mushroom might be the giant puffball. In its mature form it's as big as a football or bigger, perfectly white and round, and really can't be confused with anything else. The flesh inside is white, and it is tasty sliced and fried. Then move on to a couple from the bolete family or the ceps. The easiest to mistake are probably ordinary-looking white mushrooms: some of them are not so ordinary.

Bear in mind that it's illegal in some forests to remove mushrooms, so check with your local woodland corporation.

101.

START A FIRE WITHOUT MATCHES

People like starting fires in autumn. As the days start drawing in, it seems to be the thing to do to add comfort to our lives. There's Bonfire Night, Halloween, Diwali, all revolving around fire and light amid the encroaching darkness.

When you're lighting a fire this November, why not impress your friends with a simple trick: light a fire without matches, using a battery and some steel wool. You can also do this on a camping trip if you are stuck with wet matches.

First of all, a battery. Preferably a 9-volt battery, the square ones with the positive and negative terminals at the top. Now some steel wool. You will need the very fine kind that is sold as a pad for scouring pans, and sometimes impregnated with soap. The method is simplicity itself. Holding the pad in one hand, rub the battery terminals gently back and forth against it. Within seconds the steel wool will begin to glow red hot. This is because the battery is sending a current through the tiny filaments of the steel wool, which are getting over-excited and heating up. This isn't one of those miracles that happens after hours of patient rubbing: it happens immediately. Place some paper or dry leaves against the red-hot wires and they will burst into flame. Then add some kindling such as small sticks or twigs. Blow on it, add logs to taste, and you have a rampant bonfire going, as well as some seriously impressed friends.

You can also start a fire with an aluminium can and a chocolate bar, but believe me, it takes forever.

102.

PLANT NEW POTATOES FOR CHRISTMAS

When do you plant new potatoes? Spring? No! Potatoes can be planted at any time of the year, as long as it's not too near winter. And if you plant them in October, they'll be ready for Christmas dinner.

First of all, around mid-September, buy certified disease-resistant 'first early' seed potatoes from a garden centre or similar stockist (don't use potatoes you've bought in a grocer). Then 'chit' them. This means putting them in a warm, dark place, inside the house, for a month, and letting them pre-sprout. In mid-October, or by the end of October, they're ready to plant out.

You can plant them in tubs or in the ground, but the method is basically the same. Dig a hole five inches deep and plant each potato. Space them about a foot apart, then cover them with earth, leaving the sprouts showing above the soil. As the weather gets colder they may need to be protected from frosts, which you can do by making a cloche with horticultural fleece. They'll be OK as long as the ground doesn't freeze (which won't generally be until later in the year).

On Christmas Eve, go out into your garden and dig up your buried treasure. Your new potatoes will each be about the size of eggs. Boil them, slather them with butter and have them with your Christmas fowl or nut roast. A freshly dug-up new potato is the very tang of the awakened earth.